FEAR LESS LIVING

FEAR LESS LIVING

Ileana M. Leon

ISBN # 978-1-7371563-1-4

Scripture taken from the Holy Bible, New International Version, NIV copyright © 1973, 1978, 1984, 2011 by Biblica Inc. Used by permission.

Scripture is taken from the New King James Version®. Copyright © 1982 by Thomas Nelson. Used by permission. All rights reserved.

The information presented is the author's opinion and does not constitute any professional medical advice. The content of this book is for informational purposes only and is not intended to diagnose, treat, cure, or prevent any condition or disease.

Cover design by Tony Gonzalez

REVIEWS

Fear Less Living by Author and close friend, Ileana Leon puts words of knowledge and personal experience to paper. After reading her book, I was able to see the transformation that has occurred. This book is a dynamic display of real-life struggles. It provides support and practical exercises to assist the reader. Ileana offers much encouragement and understanding for anyone battling fear and anxiety with the hope to overcome both.

I am honored to have walked through the past 13 years with her. Reading Fear Less Living has shown me how unconditional love and prayer are powerful tools. The desire to live unstuck and unafraid can be achieved. This book is a must have for anyone crippled by fear and anxiety. As well as, family and friends that often give up or feel hopeless.

I have seen with my eyes and heard with my ears as Ileana walked this out. She is a Warrior and she has written a book to lead others to be Warriors too. Bravo!

Kim Doran
Author & Speaker
Lead, Pack Your Suitcase, Trials and Triumphs

If you are looking for a lasting antidote to anxiety and for tangible tools to pull out of your tool chest when you feel the monster of apprehension creeping into your thoughts, then this is a book for you. This author delves deeply into her own personal life to show many examples. With humor, honesty, and self awareness, she illustrates the various points about the Goliath, that is anxiety. She effectively weaves biblical truths throughout the book to instruct and inspire. Since ultimately, the true solution for anxiety is found in Scripture.

Lest you think this will be a relaxing read, know that it will be hard work. It's not a walk in the park, nevertheless, it beats the alternative of living with anxiety. I encourage you to do that work. The freedom that you will experience will be so worth it. Because YOU are so worth it!

I highly recommend this book and look forward to reading more from this author in the future.

Kiki Bacaro, MS, MHC
Master of Psychology, Mental Health Counselor

DEDICATION

Dedicated to my mother, Victoria, the bravest woman I've known.

FOREWORD

What a genial idea to have the interweaving of a workbook in the chapters of the book Fear Less Living! Also, the reader will be delighted by the fact that in this writing, our author, Ileana Leon, is supremely transparent, insightful, and humorous. Ileana reveals her inner, broken core which is common to our human family-regardless of gender.

Ileana uncovers her psychological scars. She explains the original wounds. She brought us face to face with the fears, anxieties, and phobias. She takes time to describe her pains and the thought processes that led to the decision to get help. She describes the stitching. The cauterization and the healing process. As readers, we even become acquainted with the Master Surgeon and Ultimate Healer. Her previous book, The Edge of Truth, is also an excellent book; it touched us from beyond the veil as a work of fiction.

Now, Fear Less Living catapults us close and personal. Our author delivers concrete and powerful tools for overcoming our overt and hidden phobias. As a result, we willingly concede. We open the windows of our imprisoned souls. The healing sunshine and fresh air breeze in. We venture out empowered, triumphant, and free.

Anthony Bruno

Life Coach, Pastor, Podcaster

TABLE OF CONTENTS

INTRODUCTION

When I was trying to pick a title for this book, I first thought of Fearless Living. Catchy title, but was it fitting? That title seemed more appropriate for those who intrepidly jump out of airplanes or bungee jump off cliffs. We salute your fearlessness.

Fear Less Living is written for anyone who has anxiety. The anxiety can stem from Generalized Anxiety, Health Anxiety, Panic Disorder or any other undiagnosed condition. It can come from phobias and obsessions that keep you enslaved. The book can also help the average Jane or Joe who seeks sanctuary from daily worries.

Are you really living? Or are you tip-toeing through your life too afraid to enjoy it? God gave us the gift of life. We are to experience it and savor it. Fear less living, means more living and less fearing.

Have you ever wondered what it would be like if you could take control of your fears? Wouldn't it be wonderful if you could go through the day, not necessarily fear-free, but prepared to handle the fear that comes your way? What a difference in your daily life that would make! I must warn you, if you are looking for an instant cure, a quick and painless method, close the book right now. If you are sick and tired of feeling fearful and are willing to be persistent in applying the steps outlined in this book, you will find the peace you long for.

In this book I will introduce you to the Honesty Box. I will ask you to be straightforward with all your feelings. It is there to help you remain focused on the truth and not the empathetic lies you tell yourself when you are battling fear. Along the way, I will be giving you tidbits of truth and Scripture to reflect on. You will discover the origin of fear and what you can do to disarm the culprit. You will focus on learning strategies, as well as how to reduce the symptoms and calm down the nervous system. I have devised some exercise pages for you to work on. Fighting anxiety is not a passive event. You must become an active participant in your healing.

*Please note: I don't make any guarantees implied or otherwise, about the results of the strategies, suggestions, or from the exercises you will find in this book. I share what worked for me in the hopes it helps you with your anxiety. Nevertheless, you need to understand that your success or failure will be the result of your own efforts in your particular situation. There may be other circumstances beyond my knowledge or control that can affect your outcome.

Take heart, with a little faith and hard work, by the end of this book, you too will be able to get out of the prison of fear and start the journey into Fear Less Living.

"I can do anything through Christ which strengthens me" (Philippians 4:13).

THE ORIGIN OF FEAR

Fear is an emotion. Like all emotions, it has a purpose. Fear was not known when man was first created. God did not create Adam to fear anything. He was not afraid of any of the wild animals that roamed around the Garden of Eden. As a matter of fact, Adam was given the task of naming all of them. Eve was not afraid of anything either. However, after they sinned, fear became their constant companion. It severed the close relationship they had with God and each other.

But the Lord God called to the man, "Where are you?" He answered, "I heard you in the garden and I was afraid because I was naked; so, I hid." (Genesis 3:9-10).

After Adam and Eve sinned by eating from the Tree of Knowledge of Good and Evil, they were kicked out of Eden. Outside the garden, the wild beasts were not friendly. From that point on, fear became man's survival mechanism.

From the very beginning, our bodies were designed by God to help us survive this world. Dangerous situations will produce certain biochemical reactions in our bodies. These reactions can work for our benefit when we are faced with real danger. The problem lies when we perceive fear where there is no real danger, or when we exaggerate fear due to our unrestrained thoughts. When our bodies answer that misinterpreted call, our troubles begin.

For all intent and purposes, we will call the place where you and I battle fear day in and day out, Fearville. It is the place where our enemy, Satan reigns. To the citizens of Fearville *change* is a bad word. Those who have been exiled to the not-so-glamorous city accept it without question. Fear is welcomed as an inevitable part of who you are.

In Fearville, the only thing required of you is that you remain scared. The longer you remain in Fearville, the more proficient you become in the dark art of being fearful. You become a real pro, proudly displaying the trophy list of phobias that can run a mile long. The state of affairs is always the same in Fearville. God is not welcome. He requires you to make some changes and that goes against the enemy's plans. God is perceived as illusive, detached, and even cruel. His mercy, His love, and His strength, are mere elements of a sweet fairy tale that works for others but could never work for you.

That is what you have been led to believe.

In Fearville, you might know the philosophy of a Risen Savior. You might have even professed that He lives in your heart, answered an altar call, etc. Apart from that, have you ever really trusted him with **all** your fears? You and I can say we believe in Jesus until we are blue in the face. Unless we give up the comfort of living in Fearville, we won't be able to experience His healing.

Friend, to leave Fearville one must make a conscious effort to reject the safety of the known. You must part with the familiarity of fear and instead, run into the arms of the unknown where Jesus waits patiently for you.

Then Jesus told him, "Because you have seen me you have believed; blessed are those who have not seen and yet have believed" (John 20:29).

As humans we like to think we are in control, don't we? However, life teaches us that we cannot always be in control of everything. People get sick, appointments get canceled and if you live in Florida, hurricanes happen. I could be making all sorts of plans and living out my predictable existence until the local news sounds the alarm. Soon my life will be turned upside down by the upcoming forecast.

Living in Fearville does not exempt you from change. Regardless of the fear we may have of change, it happens without our permission. From the moment we take our first breath to our last, our minds, and our bodies, undergo vital transformation. We may start as helpless babies, but we don't stay that way for long. No one has ever gone from an infant to an adult without going through some level of growth. Change, is a normal part of the God-ordained process of maturity. Now that you understand you can't avoid it, are you ready to leave Fearville?

The baggage from Fearville must remain behind. If you think you need to pack before heading out, don't. Forget what didn't work in the past, it will just bog you down. Will this be a leisurely walk out of Fearville and a straight path to freedom? No. Where you are going you will get shiny new weapons to fight. It will be a dragged-out knockdown battle. Once you cross over from Fearville to the other side, you will enjoy the sweet taste of victory. Ready to get started?

Survivor

No matter the fear
No matter the tears
You are a Survivor

No matter the tries
No matter the lies
You are a Survivor

Even through the pain
Drowning in the rain
You are a Survivor

You get up
You get down
You are a survivor

You fall
You rise
You are a Survivor

Every second, every minute
You think you are dying
You are Surviving!

STEP 1 ADMIT YOUR FEAR

For any support system to work, you must be willing to admit you have a problem. Alcoholics Anonymous and Celebrate Recovery meetings are about facing the truth. Contrary to what you may have been told, admission of what you struggle with is not weakness.

It takes courage to admit you suffer from anxiety and fear. Admitting your fears, takes away the security blanket of bravado, stirring your will and intellect. It causes you to evaluate and weigh your options. Admitting truth gives you a place to start, and a foundation to build on.

You will have to work on tearing down the walls of excuses you have built around yourself. This uncomfortable process places you inside what I will be referring to as the *Honesty Box*.

Close your eyes and use your imagination. The box has a mirror and a seat inside. Do you see it? On the next page, you will be drawing your Honesty Box. It will give you a visual reminder as you are reading this book of the decisions you are making. Additionally, it serves as a reminder of the power you have against fear and anxiety.

You do have power!

Be strong and courageous. Do not be afraid or terrified because of them, for the Lord our God goes with you; he will never leave you nor forsake you" (Deuteronomy 31:6).

WORKBOOK PAGE

INSTRUCTIONS ON HOW TO DRAW YOUR HONESTY BOX

Personalize it. Take special care to draw your box, seat, and mirror in a meaningful way. Be creative. Is your mirror round or square? What would you like it to be made of, wood, steel, gold, or silver? What shape is your box? (It does not have to be square.) The chair itself can be made of any material. Keep in mind, the seating must be comfortable. Sitting in the box needs to make you feel important. (My chair has a plush, velvet, seat because I spend a lot of time sitting on it.)

Here are some ideas to get you started:

Add your name in the space provided before the 'S.

You can draw the box and color it with colored pencils, markers, or any drawing tool you want to use.

If you don't want to draw, you can cut out a picture from a magazine and glue it to the space provided.

You can embellish it any way you like. Add stickers, shiny stars, etc.

This assignment may seem silly and childish, I assure you it's not. Don't skip it. Don't rush through it. Sometimes the simplest things make the most impact. Take your time and make it memorable.

_____'S

HONESTY BOX

Once you are inside the Honesty Box, all the excuses are gone. All the fairy tales are finished. You must accept yourself for what you are, an imperfect human being.

Inside this box, you must deal with reality. This is where you get to choose whether you want to remain where you are, or move ahead and learn constructive ways to work through your anxiety and fear.

FYI: You will be traveling on the 'road less traveled' out of Fearville. I have taken this road before, and I can testify that it is not an easy road. In the past, maybe you took this road yourself and got lost. Like me, you tried to go through it at neck-breaking speed, only to end up crashing. One time I made it to the crevice and hung on for dear life until all my energy was spent and I gave up. I went back to the comfort of the 'known.' I returned to Fearville.

If you think that my returning categorized me as hopeless, it didn't. It taught me some valuable lessons. The same lessons I will be helping you learn.

As you work through the fears, remind yourself that you have made the following choices:

I _____ suffer from anxiety and fear. I am choosing to do the following to leave Fearville: (Sign your name in the space provided)

1. I choose to allow God to work in my life

2. I choose to have faith.

3. I choose to acknowledge the truth.

4. I choose to look for a solution.

5. I choose to have hope.

6. I choose to forgive.

7. I choose to trust.

8. I choose to receive love.

9. I choose to give love.

THEN YOU WILL KNOW THE TRUTH,
AND THE TRUTH WILL SET YOU FREE.

JOHN 8:32

NOTES

STEP 2 UNDERSTAND YOUR FEAR

"For God hath <u>not</u> given us a spirit of fear, but of power, and of love, and of a sound mind"(2 Timothy 1:7). New King James Version

In the Bible, Jesus gives much significance to the destructive effects that fear can have in a person's spiritual and daily life. He tells us not to be afraid of anything because, *"The one who is in you, (God) is greater than the one who is in the world" (1 John 4:4 NIV).*

God blessed us with our spirit, our body, and our soul. He did not give us the spirit of fear. If God did not give us this spirit, who did? Satan. He is known as the adversary and Father of Lies. He is the warden in Fearville.

I can remember as if it were yesterday, the first time I experienced a full-blown panic attack. It was a year after my grandfather had passed away. I had gone into the closet to look for something when this terrifying sensation invaded my body. It felt like waves of pins and needles going up and down. My vision was fading, and everything seemed foggy, surreal. I thought I was having an allergic reaction to the mothballs in the closet. When I left the area, it worsened. I started with dizziness and nausea. My heart was beating so fast it hurt to breathe. This degree of fear could only be duplicated under the extreme circumstances of facing a horrifying creature that is ready to kill you.

I hate hospitals. You could say I have a phobia of being poked and prodded. This stems back to childhood trauma. I had a heart murmur caused by rheumatic fever and I had to travel daily to the doctor's office to be injected with Penicillin. (Penicillin shots back then would leave you limping for a few hours.) That day the fear of hospitals became secondary to the fear that I was dying. Therefore, I begged my mother to take me to the Emergency Room. I was certain that at any moment, I was going to die or pass out. Neither happened.

After that night, the spells began to plague me without warning. They would come on with such intensity, that I was sure I had some life-threatening illness. To my relief and dismay, my physical checkup came back normal. The diagnosis was panic disorder. I was given medication for the dizzy spells and some Xanax to help my frazzled nerves.

Even with the medication, the spells didn't go away. They kept coming on as a continual reminder that "they" were in control. This devastating force kept me in an exhausted state of panic. I began to avoid any place where the panic attacks had occurred. I remember dreading going into the kitchen to get a drink of water for fear it would happen again. I stopped going to the movies for the same reason. Fear became the catalyst for the vicious cycle that dominated my every move. Friends, I was stuck in Fearville and didn't even know it!

One time while visiting my neighbor, I had a feeling that something awful was going to happen. I felt an overwhelming desire to run away. After making up an excuse, I bolted out the door. My heart hammered. I coughed and gasped to take in air. I lived right next door, nevertheless, my jelly legs and dry heaving made it a hardship to get home.

When the nervous system is bombarded by an unexpected gush of adrenaline, your mind will trick you into believing that you are not safe anywhere. The haunting thoughts and symptoms will catch up with you no matter where you hide.

Through the years, I have endured hundreds of panic attacks. It is only by holding on to the promises of the risen Savior; that I have been able to keep from drowning in Fearville's murky Lake of Depression.

WORKBOOK PAGE

What does fear and anxiety keep you from doing?

_____

If you didn't have anxiety, what dreams would you pursue?

_____

How does anxiety and fear affect your relationship with others?

_____

How does anxiety and fear affect your physical health?

_____

How does anxiety and fear affect your ability to thrive in life?

_____

Today's experts will tell you that you can improve your life in any way you choose through positive thinking and tapping into your inner strength. That is what is called tapping the "god within," or as they call it in New Age terminology, "Higher Consciousness, or Divine Energy." Throughout this chapter, I will be referring to these philosophies, as the "god within."

Focusing on positive thinking alone, will only skim the surface of your problems. There is an error in this philosophy taught and preached by today's positive thinking gurus and backed up 100% by the media. It teaches that the ultimate power is found inside ourselves. According to these teachings it is by our own volition alone or achieving higher consciousness, in essence, becoming more "god" like, that we can conquer our fears. This is the fastest way to end up crashing as we make our escape out of Fearville.

Most self-help books claim you can create your own Utopia. I almost bought into it. I thought, "Hey, why not?" God does want us to have an abundant life and we are to speak good into our lives. This was all acceptable until I realized the authors of the self-help books I was reading, had left God hanging out to dry! In the quest for a personal Utopia, they had forgotten the original creator of the first and only Utopia on earth. Our Biblical ancestors forfeited the Garden of Eden with their sinful behavior. We carry the same sinful nature. What makes us think we can do any better without God?

Countless people in the media have allowed the world's philosophy to dictate their behavior. Some have ended their lives prematurely through suicide. Others live enslaved by the addictive effects of illicit drugs and alcohol. The majority of Hollywood has been marked by their multiple love affairs. Many of them end up alone battling depression. All these aesthetically beautiful people have one thing in common; they rode the roller coaster ride of the "god within." They fed their starving egos with every pleasure available.

Only to find the hunger never stopped, and the fears that plagued them never quit. They chased the elusive dream of fulfillment only to brush up against happiness for just a short time.

The "god within" system may appear to work at first because it revolves completely around you, your needs, your strengths, and your desires. Isn't it true that if you have your ego stroked enough times, you will eventually feel as invincible as a Superhero? Let's be honest here. Invigorated, renewed, and empowered by your elevated ego, you will move unhindered like a runaway freight train to annihilate your fears. Ask yourself, but at what cost?

Eventually, the thrill of victory wears off and your human strength is spent. You are left back at square one fighting the endless war against the same old enemy. Remember, fear does not get tired after the first few rounds. It just keeps on punching.

Let's look at this process of tapping the power within ourselves from a scientific point of view. Think of yourself as a deflated balloon.

When the balloon is pumped up with air. (The lies the you are told to believe) See examples below:

Ex: You are destined for success, the power is within you, you alone can conquer all!

The balloon expands filling the interior. Suddenly the walls stretch out becoming firmer and sturdier. The more air that is blown into it, the stronger it becomes until it reaches its full capacity.

Now, take a nice sharp pin and poke it. (Problems that come up in your life)

Ex: Getting fired from a job, financial difficulties, rejection from a loved one, criticism, a major panic attack, etc. What happens next?

Kaboom!

All the air inside its tight parameters could not keep it from exploding. Neither will the hot air pumped by those who peddle this egocentric belief system, help you stay in one piece. If you go through life on sheer willpower, you may advance some. (The balloon will expand.) Nevertheless, you will never reach your full potential. You will never soar. What's more, you will never know the joy of living a life that is connected to the greatest power source imaginable! Don't hinge your hopes for fear-free living on counterfeit, pretty-packaged lies. Set your eyes on the God who hung the stars in place and loves you more than you can fathom.

Authentic positive thinking is 100% backed up by God's Word. Our Heavenly Father in His divine wisdom wants us to meditate on the positive. Nowhere in the Bible does it state God wants us to be pessimistic or negative. Authentic positive thinking is backed up by science as well.

Researchers continue to explore the effects of positive thinking and optimism on health. Health benefits that positive thinking may provide include:

- Increased life span

- Lower rates of depression

- Lower levels of distress and pain

- Greater resistance to illnesses

- Better psychological and physical well-being

- Better cardiovascular health and reduced risk of death from cardiovascular disease and stroke

- Reduced risk of death from cancer

- Reduced risk of death from respiratory conditions

- Reduced risk of death from infections

- Better coping skills during hardships and times of stress i

18

To escape Fearville you must believe in yourself. A healthy self esteem is an important part of the recovery process. But it should never take the place of God. He is the infinite focal point. How much more secure you will feel knowing your greatest efforts are backed up by a loving God who wants to see you enjoying your life and all He has created. You have in your corner the best trainer that ever walked this earth, "The Champion of Champions." Can you hear the crowd going wild? I can! The whole heavenly realm rejoices!

So why do you still look so depressed? Oh yes, you don't do much smiling in Fearville, do you? Well, let's keep going. I am sure that smile will eventually reappear.

WORKBOOK PAGE

What helps you cope with your fears? Put an x next to each one that applies:

____ Food, sweets, salty

____ Sleep

____ TV

____ Prayer

____ Self-Help Books

____ Social Media

____ Shopping

____ Drinking

____ Smoking

____ Exercising

____ Working

____ Hobbies

____ Reading the Bible

____ Talking to a friend or loved one

Other _____

TRUTH FROM THE HONESTY BOX
JESUS FELT FEAR TOO

Does that statement in the Honesty Box surprise you? It did to me at first until I read the Bible looking for evidence. In Matthew 26, we learn that Jesus in His humanity was no stranger to fear. He knew the horrible ordeal of the upcoming crucifixion. There would be betrayal and abandonment by His closest friends. Even Peter, the "Rock" would deny knowing Him. Jesus prayed the cup would be removed not once but three times! (Matthew 26:39, Mark 14:36 Luke 22:42). This is the same plea, we cry out, "Lord I don't want to do this or go through this, please make it go away!"

As the Son of the Living God, Jesus in all His majesty could have decided, I don't need to do this; I can destroy mankind and start from scratch. As a human man, He could have denied the cross, claiming it was too painful. However, instead of shrinking from His responsibility, He bowed His head and told the Father, "Yet not my will, but yours be done" (Luke 22:42). That is how much you and I are loved.

It states in the Bible Jesus was sweating on the Mount of Olives, and His sweat was like droplets of blood. Luke 22:44. Perhaps at this moment His physical body was experiencing the rush of adrenaline, the heart palpitations, and the rivers of perspiration that often accompanies the emotional state of panic. It even states that an angel from heaven appeared to Him and strengthened Him. In His human flesh, His fear was so great and His depression so deep that the Lord sent a helper to Him. (Luke 22 :43).

God does not leave us alone in our anxiety and raging fear either. We have a helper. The same Holy Spirit that Jesus sent to His disciples in the Upper Room is available to us. We can have the same magnificent comforter who filled the disciples with the burning desire to boldly proclaim the Word; heal the sick and perform miracles.

The Holy Spirit is our Paraclete, (One who walks beside you to help you). The Holy Spirit can empower you to be strong in your faith when the odds are against you. When fear thinks it is the boss, you need to remind it, Holy Spirit is in the house. Whoop! Whoop!

Jesus knows exactly what you are feeling when you are faced with a fearful situation. Most of all, He knows what it feels like to panic and He has experienced depression. "My soul is overwhelmed with sorrow to the point of death..." (Mark 14:34). How deep Jesus' depression must have been, everything must have seemed hopeless! Jesus' heart was so broken He wanted to die. Haven't you wished at one time or another God would just take you? I know I have.

You can claim biblical promises when your faith is put to the test by the symptoms of fear and anxiety. God promised He would never leave us or forsake us (Deuteronomy 31:6).

Jesus wants to help us carry our burdens just as the Father did for Him on the Mount of Olives. Won't you let Him?

Come to me, all you who are weary and burdened, and I will give you rest. take my yoke upon you and learn from me, for I am gentle and humble in heart, and you will find rest for your souls. For my yoke is easy and my burden is light" (Matthew 11:28-30).

In this chapter, I gave you a firm foundation to build your faith on. Now we can begin to expose what fear really is and start dismantling the lies we have believed.

WORKBOOK PAGE 1a

For this exercise you will need the following:

1 blank sheet of paper

scissors

plastic bag- like the ones used to carry your groceries. You may also use a paper bag.

Think about what emotions you have felt due to the anxiety and fear you have felt this past or present week. On the list below, circle all the emotions that describe how you felt. You can add any not listed below.

Angry

Bitter

Disgusted

Resentful

Irritated

Defensive

Jealous

Depressed

_____

_____

_____

WORKBOOK PAGE 1b

Pick up the blank sheet 8 1/2 by 11.

Fold in it half. (Top touching the bottom.)

Fold in it half again. (Top to bottom.)

Fold over left to right.

Open it up. You should have 8 creases forming 8 squares.

Write on each square one emotion you circled. It is okay if you have less than 8.

Cut out each square.

Fold the squares. (Refer back to instructions for folding the sheet of paper.)

Keep them folded.

Throw them in your bag.

Put away the bag. (You will be using it again.)

There are traumas and negative experiences where we have been hurt by others. The past influences how we react when we are confronted with similar circumstances in the present. These become what therapists call our triggers.

A trauma trigger is a psychological stimulus that prompts involuntary recall of a previous traumatic experience. 2

It is understandable if you feel others are to blame for your triggers and all the anxiety that plagues you. Holding the person(s) responsible for the hurt that they caused is justifiable. I would be doing you a disservice if I don't tell you that the blame game will not help you get out of Fearville.

The "blame game" does not provide a haven for you to express your grief. Yes, there is comfort in nursing your wounds. Having someone to blame shifts the focus off your brokenness. In this state of mind, all you are doing is dumping fresh manure on the root of bitterness. This root will propagate like wildfire in Fearville. Bitterness can then grow unhindered until it ultimately chokes the life out of you. The person causing the hurt ends up holding you hostage by the hatred that is consuming you. In my case, that person continued to live his life unaware of the mess he had made in mine.

Forgiveness is the only weed killer that works on blame. Forgiving yourself and forgiving others hacks away at the bitterness that blocks the exit out of Fearville. We will unpack the topic of forgiveness in depth in a later chapter.

In certain circles, it is more common to hear of people suffering from a physical ailment, than to hear that someone is having psychological problems. When you do hear such news, mostly it is being said in hushed tones. It usually comes from the merry-go-round of loose lips than from the person's mouth. What may have started as a small episode of depression or anxiety, the gossip mill now has labeled it, a severe mental breakdown of epic proportion. Careless words can do more damage than good. God warns us to be careful when we remove our tongue from its sheath.

I went to a healing service years ago. Many people were pouring onto the altar. Most problems were physical. They ranged from sprained ankles to cancer. Standing in my pew, I felt a tug to go up to the altar. Shame kept holding me back. Satan kept telling me, *it is not physical; you have no right to ask for help. You can't go up because you don't deserve a blessing. Look at how you let fear dominate you. You are a pathetic excuse for a Christian.* Can you see the negative tape playing in my head?

Standing there, surrounded by loving people that I knew, I felt so alone and unworthy. Thankfully, my husband's encouraging words overpowered the thoughts and I went up to the altar. There was someone up there whom I had heard suffered from anxiety too, yet we had never spoken about it. As you probably know, this is not a topic easily woven into a conversation.

When I finally got my turn in front of the pastor, he said, "You are at the foot of Calvary." Standing there, bogged down by all the condemnation Satan was hurling at me, I imagined how Christ must have felt nailed to that cross.

Jesus felt condemnation from every angle. He heard the mocking laughter of the crowd. Those He trusted had fled. I was reminded that Jesus carried not only our physical illnesses but our psychological and emotional ones as well. He carried them on his whip-torn flesh.

"He himself bore our sins" in his body on the cross, so that we might die to sins and live for righteousness; "by his wounds you have been healed" (1 Peter 2:24).

What the Lord was telling me that day was, *Look up! See the flesh and bone human on the cross? You are not alone in your suffering. I have been there too. Instead of trying to beat this thing on your own, surrender it and I will not hesitate to help you.*

Did you notice that the Scripture says, *have been?* It is written in the past tense. It has already been done! What right do you have to come into God's presence, to kneel at the foot of the cross, with your fears? Every right! You are God's highly esteemed creation. You are His priceless masterpiece. The enemy does not want you to know that you are loved. You were bought and paid for by the sacrificial blood of Jesus. It is up to you whether you accept this or not.

WORKBOOK PAGE

THE GOLDEN RULES OF THE HONESTY BOX

- *ADMIT YOU HAVE A PROBLEM. (ACKNOWLEDGE YOUR WEAKNESS)*

- *BE WILLING TO BREAK DOWN ALL EXCUSES AND WALLS YOU HAVE BUILT AROUND YOU.*

- *BE WILLING TO DEAL WITH THE REAL YOU, FLAWS AND ALL*

(You must be willing to see yourself from a realistic perspective with no excuses and no pretenses.)

Picture yourself inside your box. Take some slow, deep breaths and bring your shoulders down. Remember shoulders are not your earrings.

Open your eyes and look at the question below. Don't rush to answer it. Think about what you have read and ask God to show you the truth.

Is there someone (including yourself) or something that you feel is keeping you from seeking help for your anxiety? Write the answer below.

_____

TRUTH FROM THE HONESTY BOX
GUILT CAN MIMIC GODLY CONVICTION

September 11, 2001, terrorists attacked our country. The Twin Towers crumbled and with this attack, thousands of people lost their lives. Heroes emerged from the ashes and many turned their eyes toward God for the very first time. Many people volunteered, gave blood, gave money, and traveled to minister to our hurting brothers and sisters in New York.

During this crisis, I ran across someone who had been contemplating going on a mission trip to NY before this happened. Joy confided in me that she felt emotionally unstable, due to a traumatic circumstance that had occurred in her personal life.

When she asked her church to support her decision not to go, it was not well received. They knew she was Bipolar and this kind of stress could compromise her mental health; still they expected her to go. This church falls into the category of churches that don't understand that mental illness is not a sin or an excuse. It is not caused by a lack of faith. Those with mental health or neurological disorders deserve the same empathy as those who have cancer, diabetes, or heart conditions. Mental illness is still an illness.

When Joy asked my advice on this matter of going to NY, I told her to pray and ask God if it was His will for her to go. Even after praying, this woman had no peace. She feared having another mental breakdown due to the stress of dealing with the devastating destruction and loss of lives.

Should she go just to please everyone else? Could she bring any hope to anyone when she was living in a depressive-manic state herself? This situation, in addition to other incidents that had occurred in what she expected to be a safe zone; caused her anxiety to double. In this microwave society, nobody took the time to peel back the layers of Joy's fears and see what was going on. Instead, they pointed fingers and judged her. Can you see how Satan blurred the lines between guilt and conviction? His real intent all along was to discourage this woman from attending church and make her wary of other Christians. What had started as an opportunity for ministry became another reason for fearing the fellowship of believers. It took this woman years before she could feel confident enough to step foot inside a church again, and a few more to begin regular attendance.

This unnecessary anxiety was provoked by Satan using well-meaning people who wanted her to get over her depression and fear. When you hear, "Get over it," Run!

There is a season for everything. Don't feel guilty if during this season you cannot handle doing nursery duty at your church or being on the planning committee for your best friend's surprise party. There will be other seasons when you can participate. If you don't take the time to meet your emotional and physical needs first, you could miss out on a blessing God had for you all along.

When we can't physically help, there is always one position that is waiting to be filled. It is the most humbling of all positions. There is no outward recognition, no material rewards, and no pat on the back. Even so, oh, how God honors that position! Did you know that Prayer Warriors are in high demand around the clock, 365 days a year?

Prayer is powerful. It is something that anyone can do at any given time. Interceding for others takes on a different meaning when we see how important it is. Prayer Warriors are part of our defense team, and without these devoted people praying behind the scenes, life would be a lot harder for all of us.

In a Women of Faith conference, I heard Patsy Claremont say, "Our minds can be a factory of fear or a factory of faith." This was a profound statement since Patsy herself suffered from Agoraphobia and was home bound for some time. When I hear stories like that coming out of the mouths of Pillars of the Faith, it brings the issue of fear into perspective. With our knees trembling and our mind whirling, we can still be used by God.

TRUTH FROM THE HONESTY BOX
THE WORLD WILL KEEP ON TURNING EVEN IF I AM NOT THE ONE MAKING IT TURN

Guilt-induced fear can masquerade itself as something noble in the "Yes" person. We are the ones who just cannot say "no" to anyone or anything for fear that we won't be liked. To us, saying no means we will be letting someone down and that will make us sick to our stomachs. We are what psychologist label as "type A" personalities. We are the ones driven to accomplish, regardless of what it does to us in the end.

The more difficult traits that come with a Type A personality definition include:

Chronic competitiveness

Impatience

Aggression

Hostility

Type A's have tendencies to engage in urgent and achievement-oriented behavior, people with a Type A personality may feel more stressed or develop stress-related disorders.3

Those with Type A personalities carry a lot of guilt, especially when our emotional and physical limitations don't allow us to accomplish all we are asked to do. We have agendas filled to the brim. We fill our already busy schedule with good deeds that we must do, programs we must attend, and activities we must participate in. We are the owners of a never-ending To Do list, even if it kills us.

Should we chuck it all and sit home eating chocolate and watching cute animals on YouTube? As stress-free, as it sounds, becoming a hermit is not the answer. So, what is?

Meet Margaret. She is bright and friendly, and like us, a very busy person. Daily, she chauffeurs her two kids to school before embarking on the task of running her home business. She takes phone calls, fills in orders, and troubleshoots for her clients. All this while keeping tabs on her wandering toddler. Margaret also attends her local University twice a week in hopes of attaining her Master's Degree. She is very active in her church. The young woman sings in the choir, teaches Sunday school, cook meals for the sick, and leads a women's Bible Study on Friday nights. Whenever the nursery is understaffed or a ministry needs last-minute baking, Margaret is the first name that pops up. "Call Marge, she is always available. I tell you that girl is an angel in disguise!"

Unfortunately, this little angel has a very big problem. Her priorities are out of whack and it's catching up to her. Margaret is very unhappy. Most of the things she volunteers for have lost their appeal. She still does them; however, the enthusiasm is gone. Not to mention, she's been suffering from stomach problems and panic attacks. The doctor says it's caused by too much stress, even so, Margaret just feels so guilty when people call. She's short-tempered with her family and cries easily. Poor Margaret is headed for a nervous breakdown, Margaret is guilt driven by the fear of letting anyone down.

Then you have those who no matter how much they accomplish, feel it is not enough. Meet Mr. Over-Achiever, he works long hours and skips lunch to meet deadlines. He's part of the volunteer pool at church. On the weekends if he is not fixing something for a widow, he is mentoring kids out in the community. Meals are eaten in haste. His digestion suffers and he wonders why he has insomnia.

When will we understand it is not healthy for us to be everything to everybody? *I thought it was our Christian responsibility to volunteer and help when we are needed?* It is. We are to volunteer our services for the good of others. Biblically that part does not change. What we must check out is the origin of our drive. That's where it can get very sticky and bring on lots of anxiety.

WARNING: This ride will get bumpy.

WHEN I SAY YES OR NO, AM I FEELING CONVICTED OR GUILTY?

Is your answer to glorify God above all else? Or is it a sense of guilt? Do you think people won't like you if you say no? Are you afraid God will love you less if you don't sing in the choir this Easter or help with the Food Drive at your child's school? Or are you trying to atone for some sin you are still carrying around? I know these questions make you uncomfortable. However, living in denial hinders mental and spiritual growth.

The biblical sisters, Martha and Mary, are the perfect examples of fear of judgment vs. freedom from condemnation. Martha and Mary opened their home to Jesus, their friend, and teacher. Martha ran around cooking, cleaning, and picking up. She was making everything perfect for her house guest. I mean, wouldn't you want everything shiny and clean if Jesus the Messiah, was visiting you? I would be freaking out! I'd be taking a toothbrush to my floor tiles, praying they end up looking like the tiles in a heavenly mansion. I would not be happy if my sister did nothing except listen to Jesus while I ran around like a chicken with my head cut off.

Could it be that at the crux of my cleaning spree resides fear - the fear that if my house was not picture perfect, then Jesus would not love me or accept me, or think I was a slob? Is that the same fear that keeps you from inviting someone over unless your house looks like it belongs in a home and garden magazine?

The Word goes on to record that Mary never bothered to lift a finger to help her stressed-out sister. Martha became so upset that she tattled.

"... Martha was distracted by all the preparations that had to be made. She came to him and asked, Lord, don't you care that my sister has left me to do the work by myself? Tell her to help me! Martha, Martha, the Lord answered, you are worried and upset about many things, but few things are needed - or indeed only one. Mary has chosen what is better and it will not be taken away from her" (Luke 10:40-42).

Okay, that hit too close to home. What was it Jesus wanted from these women? Was He putting a stamp of approval on laziness? Absolutely not. His reply had nothing to do with housework. It was about His love for her. He wanted Martha to concentrate her efforts on what would edify and feed her soul. The mundane tasks of chasing away dust bunnies, or polishing the good china could never compare to hearing His teachings.

We can glean from Mary's perspective that she felt no guilt doing the right thing. Even if that meant not finishing the household tasks that were pressing. She understood the importance of the choice she had made and would not be swayed by the guilt Martha was trying to inflict upon her.

Loved ones, friends, clergy, and activity leaders, inadvertently can make us feel guilty when we say "no." In their crusade to find volunteers, they forget not everyone should be doing the job. However, we shouldn't point fingers. There are valid reasons why they embark on this rushed job of recruitment.

The reason is a catch-22. Most churches and civic activities have to beg for individuals to volunteer. In turn, those who really can't, end up volunteering out of guilt. They take on the load of those who could do it if they would set their priorities straight. Nobody wins this way, and the end result is burned-out volunteers who are teetering between two and three activities while trying to run their household.

WORKBOOK PAGE 1a

You read about different personality types and what drives them. Fill in the blank with a personality type that describes you best.

_____

Are you a Mary or a Martha?

_____

Mary – Able to put aside tasks, worries, and fears of rejection.

Martha – Unable to put aside tasks, filled with worry about being rejected and fears of not measuring up.

If you chose Martha, we have some work to do. Marthas are not settled in their spirit. They fear disapproval.

What steps can you take to become a Mary?

_____

_____

_____

_____

WORKBOOK PAGE 1b

For this exercise you will need the following:

The plastic bag where you wrote the negative emotions that come with your fears.

1 blank sheet of paper

Scissors

Pick up 1 blank sheet 8 1/2 by 11.

Fold it in half. (Top touching the bottom)

Fold it in half again. (Top to bottom)

Fold it over from left to right

Open it up. You should have 8 creases forming 8 squares.

Write the words: Blame, Guilt, Shame, and Condemnation (one emotion per square) You should have 4 squares left.

Cut out each square you filled out.

Fold the squares. (Refer back to the original instructions for folding the sheet of paper)

Throw the folded papers in your bag.

Throw the paper with the 4 blank squares that are left, in your bag.

(You will be using it again.)

COME TO ME ALL WHO ARE HEAVY LADEN,
AND
I WILL GIVE YOU REST.

MATTHEW 11:28

NOTES

STEP 3 ACCEPT YOURSELF

TRUTH FROM THE HONESTY BOX

FEAR WILL DISTORT THE PICTURE
OF WHO YOU REALLY ARE

Did you know that everyone in Fearville has low self-esteem? It is very hard to like yourself when you feel trapped by fear all the time. You question yourself day and night, *what is wrong with me?* When you look in the mirror all you see is a defeated weakling. You magnify the tiniest imperfection, blowing it out of proportion. Then Satan will remind you of the perfect bad memory to substantiate your observation. It could be words said in haste by an angry parent, words like, "You will never amount to anything," or titles and labels that replay repeatedly in your mind in a loop. Even a stranger's unkind words can cause real damage if you internalize them. Satan's goal is for you to become brainwashed by the negativity and fall prey to self-loathing. Once you are convinced you are worthless, you become easy prey.

When I was fifteen, I had dreams of becoming a famous fashion designer, hence the idea for my fictional novel, On the Edge of Truth. I admit it; I was one of those crazy people who wanted to have my name stitched on the back pocket of a pair of jeans. Imagine that! I longed to be in the spotlight, on the other hand, I suffered terribly from Inferiority Complex. I pictured myself as a private designer working feverishly in some obscure location, creating the most beautiful gowns. My skewed, subconscious rationale was as follows: accomplish something big and you will like yourself again. Others will too. I foolishly thought that by becoming famous I could obtain recognition and it would erase all the memories of the rejection I had suffered the previous years.

Fear can make you dislike yourself. It lies to you. Have you been to the fair and stood staring at yourself in one of those funky mirrors? Those mirrors are made to distort your image. You can sit, stand, jump, and wave your arms, nevertheless, the image you see is always distorted. It's either too fat or too skinny. It can make a normal person look like a giant with a disproportionated head or a stumpy-looking creature straight out of J.R.R Tolkien's *The Lord of the Rings.4*

To correct the distortion, you need to find a mirror that works properly. Like the one, you have in your bathroom. Unfortunately, not even that mirror will tell you the whole truth. If you look close enough, you will find something you dislike about yourself. Don't feed into it. Make it a priority not to listen to your mental mirror.

As a teenager, my first experience with love proved to be devastating. The guy I was dating was emotionally abusive. He was an expert at Gaslighting.

Psychologists use the term "gaslighting" to refer to a specific type of manipulation where the manipulator is trying to get someone else (or a group of people) to question their reality, memory, or perceptions.5

My first boyfriend made sure I always knew how unattractive I was and how he was doing me a favor by dating me. He was irrationally jealous and manipulative. I tried to end the relationship; he coerced me into staying. He would point his father's gun at my head and later play on my sympathies. He would tell me that he would kill himself with that same gun if I left him. Fear of what he could do to me or himself kept me from leaving him. I must confess; my deepest fear was never finding someone who could love me for who I was.

After a year, he got bored, and through God's unfailing grace, he let me go. In retrospect, any other person would have been thrilled to be free. Instead, the breakup caused me to go into a depressive state for months. I didn't want to eat; all I did was cry. Those were all signs of dysfunction.

When you are involved in an abusive relationship, Satan uses that fear and twists it around until it becomes grotesquely attractive. After you break off the relationship, you may even go through withdrawal symptoms just like when you are kicking a bad habit. You find yourself longing to be with this person. You start to believe everything is your fault. *Maybe, if I didn't behave a certain way? If I didn't make him so angry?* You would rather suffer all kinds of indignities than have to face the fear of being alone with no one to love you.

Those who have not walked in the victim's shoes cannot understand how a person can stay with someone that mistreats them. I am not a licensed psychologist, still I have read enough psychology books to know that each Gaslighting encounter chips away a part of the victim's identity. Someone who has lost all self-worth would rather suffer the consequences of the abuse than be rejected. As sick as it may sound, with each verbal or physical attack, the victim's existence is still being acknowledged. The person loses all capability to make any decisions. They are frustrated, afraid, and feel hopelessly chained to the abuser.

Have you ever written a love letter to someone? It does not necessarily have to be romantic. It could have been written to your children, family, or friends to show them how much you care. Have you ever received a love letter or a thank you card? Those give us fuzzy, warm feelings, don't they?

It's no secret our self-esteem suffers many blows during our lifetime. The longer we are on planet Earth the more likely we suffer letdowns and are at the receiving end of insults and negativity. If we are givers, we also get depleted by pouring ourselves into others. Sometimes that task comes with no outward appreciation. I think it is about time we do something to raise our self-esteem.

WORKBOOK PAGE 1a

You are going to write a love letter. The recipient is going to be someone worthy of your admiration. So far this is a piece of cake. Well, I am not done with the directions. Take a deep breath. The recipient of this letter is YOU!

Before you throw the book away, hear me out. If you have trouble doing this, pretend you are writing to someone you truly care about. In this letter, you are to include the POSITIVE attributes you have. You can add awesome things you are proud of, and characteristics you like about yourself, both physical and personality-wise.

Dear _____,

_____

_____

_____

_____

_____

_____

_____

With Sincere Admiration,

_____

Circle all the positive words you have used to describe yourself.

WORKBOOK PAGE 1b

2nd letter. The recipient of this letter is your Creator, God. Include a thank you in the letter for all the positive traits and accomplishments that you circled in the letter to yourself.

Dear_____

_____

_____

_____

_____

_____

_____

_____

_____

_____

Thank you,

_____

Psychologists define Codependency as a dysfunctional relationship dynamic where one person assumes the role of "the giver," sacrificing their own needs and well-being for the sake of the other, "the taker."6

This buzzword was born in the pit of hell. There is nothing romantic or special about feeling the need to be with someone that puts you down or beats you up. We need to correct what society has brainwashed us to believe. We often believe the lie that it is "romantic" to be in love with someone who mistreats us. It is very difficult to remain faithful and on fire for the Lord if we are still sporting physical or emotional black and blues.

I ask you, how can you or I as part of the body of Christ, be presented without stain, wrinkle, or blemish? (Ephesians 5:25-27). It is not possible. These scars we are left with leave us with resentment and hatred, which will restrict our spiritual growth. Broken bones and wrath filled words can produce damage for a lifetime.

"In this same way, husbands ought to love their wives as their own bodies. He who loves his wife loves himself. After all, no one ever hated their own body, but they feed and care for their body, just as Christ does the church—for we are members of his body" Ephesians 5:28-30).

As a child, Mireya was easily disturbed by school exams and anything that affected her home life with her parents. She believes a lot of her problems stem from her insecurities and her parents' over protection.

"I think the trigger is insecurity. When you are insecure about yourself your mind can play a lot of tricks and tell you negative things. That is why a person needs to control their mind."

Mireya, like most women, believed in every little girl's dream of falling in love and living happily ever after. She married with the commitment of forever firmly planted in her mind. Marriage for Mireya was sacred, so when she was thrust into the whirlwind of abuse, she panicked. She was convinced that she would be dishonoring God by divorcing her husband. Therefore, she continued putting up with his verbal and physical abuse. The last straw came when he simply abandoned her and moved away with the excuse to find a better job. He would come on weekends at first, and then his abuse intensified.

When Mireya mentioned going to marriage counseling, he refused. He made no effort to remedy the situation or even find a suitable place where they could move into and work on their problems together. She turned to the church and after much deliberation and counseling, she was given the green light to file for divorce.

"I went to a retreat and a priest told me that God does not want us to be in an abusive relationship, where someone is humiliating you and treating you badly. The first time a man hits a woman or emotionally abuses her, the marriage is broken. God does not want us to be in that kind of situation. God wants us to be happy. Marriage is not easy. One thing is having problems, and another is being abused."

God freed the Israelites out of Egypt. That is how we know God does not want you to be enslaved by a tyrannical person. Just because you are dating or married to this person does not give them the right to abuse you. It does not matter how much you want the relationship to work. If the abuser does not want to take responsibility for his/her wrongdoing, it is time for you to leave them.

Fear plays a centrical role in the abuse. Mireya was fearful of her husband. This fear is realistic. If you are reading this and find yourself fearing for your life or the life of your children, please find help, and get out! I have added some abuse hotline phone numbers and websites that can be found in the Resources section of this book.

"He was very tall and physically much stronger than I. I always thought he could kill me. I remember how when we had arguments, he would yell and humiliate me. I didn't want to say something back that could make him angrier. I was afraid he would grab a knife or something sharp and kill me."

Can you hear Satan laughing? He is enjoying her terror.

"When someone constantly puts you down, you start to feel like garbage. You feel like you don't deserve to be happy or even alive. Then when God steps in and heals your broken heart, you feel like a princess."

Now that is the kind of self-esteem Satan cannot touch!

"There is no fear in love. But perfect love drives out fear, because fear has to do with punishment. The one who fears is not made perfect in love" (1 John 4:18).

Years ago, I attended a retreat. They did an exercise that changed the way I viewed myself. We were told to listen to a song as if God was speaking to us. It was a deeply moving experience when I heard the lyrics as if coming straight out of my Heavenly Father's mouth. The title of the song was *Just the Way You Are, by Billy Joel.* It spoke volumes to my teenage heart. By the end of the retreat, I had a different view of who God was. He was not just up there counting all my mistakes. He was not shaking his head in disapproval or disbelief. He loved me just the way I was, flaws and all!

Friend, God loves you regardless of whether you can carry on a conversation with Him or just stutter out a few simple words full of honesty and pain. It does not matter how you communicate, just be sincere with your Creator. He sees your potential. He fuels you with dreams and goals. God will give you whatever skills you will need to succeed, *if* you are doing it for His glory. That is the key. He loves you and knows ahead of time what needs to be accomplished. How then can you have a fulfilled life, if you have no confidence in yourself?

If we stay in Fearville we will go around moping and whining, scared out of our wits by the mere rustling of a leaf. Satan would love that. Well, let's not give him the satisfaction.

When your self-esteem is high, Depression and anxiety don't have anything to sink their teeth into. You are removing their power by accepting the truth of who you are. It does not matter what anyone has said, or is still saying about you. It matters what God says about you because He is the one who loves you unconditionally.

WORKBOOK PAGE 1a

Sit in a quiet place. You can light a candle if you like.

Close your eyes.

Talk to God. Ask Him to lead you to the song He has for you.

Research. Go on YouTube, Pandora, or even browse through your old 45s.

Listen. Look for uplifting, edifying words.

*You will know when you find the right song because you will hear His words speaking to you through the lyrics.

Write the lyrics that speak to you below:

Song Title_____

_____

_____

_____

_____

_____

_____

_____

Make it a daily habit to listen to this song, preferably when you first wake up. Before you know it, your perception of who you are and who God says you are will become evident. When it does, get ready, God is calling you out of Fearville.

WORKBOOK PAGE 1b

For this exercise you will need the following:

Sheet of paper with the cut-outs you previously used. You should have 4 blank squares left.

The plastic bag where you placed the negative emotions that come with your fears.

Directions:

Write the word *Unloved* in one square.

Write the word *Unworthy* in the other.

Pick 2 other words that describe how anxiety makes you feel and write them in the remaining blank squares.

Cut out each square you filled out.

Fold the squares. (Refer back to the original instructions for folding the sheet of paper.)

Keep them folded.

Throw them in your bag. You will be using it again.

The world needs all kinds of people. It needs extroverted people. Those are the ones with such a zest for life and a passion for their calling that they are not afraid to preach the gospel to anyone at any given moment. From the start, Paul persecuted the Christians like a renegade mercenary. After his encounter with Jesus, God used all of Paul's boldness to bring many into His kingdom.

My son, Joel, happens to be an extroverted Evangelist. When the Holy Spirit sets his heart on fire, his fear of rejection and failure is gone. He passionately proclaims the Good News without a second thought. My daughter, Katerina, is an extrovert too. She has no problem talking non-stop with anyone. She is very comfortable teaching her Sunday school class or singing in front of a crowd. What can I say? My children are the life of the party!

My husband, Frank, is the ringleader of that talkative bunch. He is the man who is on a first-name basis with everyone in our town. It was during our honeymoon that I discovered the extent of his popularity. We had just arrived at the airport in Newark for our honeymoon. During the flight, I had been teasing my husband that New Jersey was *my* turf. After all, I had grown up in the Garden State. I had it in the bag. I was convinced he would not know a single living soul except for my family whom he had previously met.

We got to the rental car counter. Lo and behold, the car rental agent knew my husband. As a matter of fact, she had worked with him! Now what are the odds? She had been transferred from Budget Rental Car in Miami, Florida six months ago! Friends, never bet against an extrovert, they know everybody!

God has made us all unique, wonderful, and gifted for the job He has in store for us. Knowing who you are in Christ and your place in this world, will give you a sense of security like no other. If you have that loud, magnetic voice that draws people to you, don't waste it.

Mary, the mother of Jesus, was a Proverbs 31 woman. I gathered from written accounts that she was an introvert. She was not portrayed as someone who constantly voiced her opinion. Mary did not go around ruffling the feathers of important dignitaries. She spoke up only when she deemed it necessary. Mostly, she stayed in the backdrop, allowing her son the center stage. She had a quiet strength, perfected by the experience of mothering the Savior of the world. This virtuous woman radiated wisdom and determination. Her presence and her sacrificial life brought hope and peace to the Disciples.

If you fall into this category, don't be misled, thinking you are not needed. Only you have that signature softness, of one who knows how to utilize their words like a surgeon's delicate instrument. Your words alone can perform life-saving surgery on the withering heart of that lonely soul.

I am an introvert by design. It is easier for me to sit back quietly and fade into the wallpaper. Normally, I do not like to make waves. I rather stay silent and remain still, as the world turns in its fallen state. Except, people's souls can't be swept under the rug. Helpless people need a voice.

As an author, I have had to step outside my comfort zone and become that voice. However, it is not my job to copy those boisterous voices, booming through the world, winning thousands of souls for Christ. Instead, I am called to hone in on my readers. Precious people like yourself, that struggle with insecurity and fear. I chose to listen to those desperate hearts searching for help. My contribution is valuable even if it is delivered through a smaller voice. I know God is pleased with it. If He calls me to greater things, He will provide the megaphone. Don't be surprised if He provides one for you too!

WORKBOOK PAGE

Do you consider yourself an introvert or an extrovert?

_____

Google all the POSITIVE traits that coincide with your choice.

Write them below:

_____   _____

_____   _____

_____   _____

Write a paragraph about how your personality can be a blessing to others. Ex: I am an introvert. I am very observant. I pick up on subtle things others may miss. When I do speak, my words tend to be right on target. I am intuitive to what others may need.

_____

_____

_____

_____

_____

_____

TRUTH FROM THE HONESTY BOX

YOU ARE NOT AN ISLAND
IF YOU WANT A BLESSING
BE A BLESSING FIRST

Sometimes we want to shut the world out because the fear of rejection is so overwhelming. If Satan can make us cold and insensitive, we have allowed him to climb one more step in his plan to make us ineffective to help others.

In the Bible, it says that we are to pray for each other. It does not say you are to carry any burden alone. Fear of rejection is not an excuse for not following God's Word. I am not saying go stand up in front of the pew on Sunday morning or at your workplace, and yell at the top of your lungs, "I suffer from panic attacks!" That would be ludicrous. Don't be surprised if you are wrestled to the ground and someone pours a gallon of holy oil on you.

All humor aside, ask the Lord to send you someone who you could learn to trust with the battle you are facing. Ask God for someone who has wisdom and can pray for you. You will need someone with backbone who is not going to sugarcoat your situation out of pity. Someone who will hold you accountable and see through your excuses and not let you off the hook. I am blessed with friends who keep me moving forward when I want to quit.

It does not stop there. You too can be a truth teller to others who are being manipulated by the lies of anxiety. God does not call us to be self-absorbed in our own misery. Your anxiety will be lower when you spend less time worrying about your own needs and more time concentrating on the needs of others.

The key word is *action*. Send a card to a friend, visit, make a meal for someone that's sick, or even a simple phone call will do. It will it be good for them, and it will help cut down on your internalizing.

WHEN IT IS YOUR TURN TO BE THE EAR, DON'T BECOME THE MOUTH. Don't sit there and cloud the other person's day with a detailed inventory of your illness or problems. Put your recent fears, aches, and pains on the back burner, and actively listen. Sympathizing is okay, just be careful not to fall into the temptation of airing out your version of how much you think life stinks. Don't compete against this person for the title of "World's Greatest Sufferer." You are there to GIVE support, not drown this individual with your own sob story.

You may think I am being cruel, after all, you are suffering too. I am reminding you of a simple fact, dating back to your preschool days. YOU HAD YOUR TURN, NOW IT'S SOMEONE ELSE'S TURN. This person needs to know you are listening and are genuinely interested in THEIR pain. As a result, you will have forgotten for a while your burdens, and brought a little sunshine into someone's day. Doesn't that make you feel good?

If you are lonely and need support, there are many support groups out there. They range from internet chat rooms to small local groups. Likewise, you can check with your church for support. One word of caution when using the Internet and other sources, make sure you don't end up in a support group that is a dumping ground for complainers.

When I got diagnosed with Fibromyalgia and Chronic Fatigue, I joined a local support group. The information they provided was helpful. The problem was, after I went home, I felt worse. I cried more, and within weeks I fell into a deep depression. I noticed that after information was passed out and reviewed, all we did was complain. This externalizing is healthy to a point, unless it becomes the main attraction of every meeting. Constant complaining can do more harm than good. This "woe is me" attitude was making me a victim of my disease.

Through a friend, I became a part of a wonderful Christian support group. Those ladies were victory seekers. They search through the scriptures like desert wanderers looking for water. This group had speakers who had professional knowledge of the subject. There was a rule established by our leader that made me want to keep attending the meetings. She told us that it was the responsibility of those who were having a good week, to encourage the ones having a bad week. Prayers, laying of hands, and meditation on God's Word helped us all. I would come home refreshed because I knew God was with me, and my sisters in Christ were only a phone call away.

If you cannot find a support group, you can start your own. With a little imagination, some initiative, and most of all God's leading, you can do it. Don't be discouraged if only one person shows up. Keep inviting people.

If you build it, he (they) will come." As stated in the movie," Field of Dreams 7

Today, technology allows people to connect in many ways. If you are home bound, and have access to a computer or smartphone, you can connect to other like-minded individuals. They have free apps you can download such as Clubhouse, Facebook, Instagram, Twitter, and many more. You can sample support groups until you find the right fit for your schedule and your needs.

WORKBOOK PAGE 1a

Look up three support groups for anxiety and fear on your phone or computer. (If you have a specific mental health diagnosis you can search for that).

Write the name of each group and the link where you found it in the space below.

_____

_____

_____

Visit the three groups and see where you feel most comfortable.

Circle the group you feel most comfortable with. Spend 1 week involved with them. If it is not what you are looking for, try the other groups.

Introvert: Step out of your shell.

• Text: someone to let them know you are thinking of them.

• Call: a friend or relative you don't normally call and speak to them on the phone.

• Visit or Invite: a friend, neighbor, or family member you don't hang out with often. Or someone you know that is sick or can't get out to socialize.

Extrovert: Invite someone that is usually quiet or reserved.

Let them do the talking. Don't try to fix or give opinions unless asked. If they won't speak, ask open-ended questions. Open-ended questions are question that require thought and cannot be simply answered by yes or no.

Ex. Why did you like the ending in that movie? What did you do today? What is your favorite food?

*If you notice the answers are short, ask further questions to get them to elaborate.

Ex. I know you told me you have many memories of your graduation day. What is your favorite memory from that day?

*Everyone likes to feel wanted or needed.

Ex. I know how good you are at computers. It be great if you could give me a hand on that on-line presentation I have to create.

Ex. You are the person I have been looking for. I love that vegetarian dish you made. Would you teach me how to make it? I will bring the ingredients.

WORKBOOK PAGE 1b

Before you finish this chapter, you must get rid of the enemy's tools that have been holding you hostage in Fearville.

For this exercise you will need: The paper bag you have been using and a permanent marker.

Directions:

Open your bag.

Take out every piece of folded-up paper.

Unfold each one.

Lie them face up on a flat surface.

Look at them.

Read each one.

All these negative, damaging emotions are strongholds that keep you enslaved. There is freedom from them. These punishing emotions were nailed on the cross when Jesus died. We are not supposed to live holding on to any of them.

Draw a large cross over each one of them with your permanent marker. All these lies are now under the cross of Jesus. You don't have to carry them around anymore!

WORKBOOK PAGE 1c

Write your name on the blank when you are ready to declare your freedom from these damaging emotions.

I _____declare that ALL my negative emotions are under the cross of Jesus.

Toss all these emotions into the bag.

Close the bag.

Throw the bag away. You can throw the bag in the trash or you can burn it.

Mark this day on your calendar. Write it in the space provided.

_____

This is the day you let go of the negative emotions that have weighed you down.

Do something nice for yourself and celebrate! Write how you are planning to reward yourself below:

_____

FOR YOU CREATED MY INMOST BEING;

YOU KNIT ME TOGETHER IN MY MOTHER'S WOMB.

I PRAISE YOU BECAUSE I AM FEARFULLY AND WONDERFULLY MADE

YOUR WORKS ARE WONDERFUL,

I KNOW THAT FULL WELL.

PSALM 139:13-14

NOTES

STEP 4 FACE YOUR FEAR

TRUTH FROM THE HONESTY BOX
FEAR LESS LIVING REQUIRES ACTION

There may be times when you will need to rely on a mental health therapist to tackle your Goliath. Friend, hear me when I say there is nothing wrong with seeing a therapist.

Before COVID hit, my trusted therapist closed her business. After COVID, I had to find a new therapist to help me deal with the aftermath of the Pandemic. To say I had trust issues with Mental Health professionals was an understatement. According to my clouded interpretation, my therapist had abandoned me and left me to fend for myself during the roughest time in my life. I never stopped to think that the woman had her own life to live.

COVID had people going to therapy in droves. Finding a therapist who accepted new patients was not an easy task. I found one who was doing Telehealth video therapy. In the first months of therapy, I almost quit going to her because she was so different from anyone I had seen before. She didn't speak much. She let me do all the talking. I thought it was strange that from the beginning she had not offered any coping tools. Weeks passed, and I got the nerve to ask for tools. The conversation was redirected. This shocked me. I continued seeing her, mostly out of curiosity. Come to find out she knew me better than I knew myself. She knew she was dealing with someone who had been in therapy before and was a research fanatic.

Who was I fooling? Not my wise therapist. She knew I had all the tools I needed. I had my faith in Jesus. I knew breathing techniques and grounding techniques. I also had a variety of tools I had picked up on my own. This included tips and strategies that I had gleaned from mental health books and articles. I could have very well been a therapist myself. (If only I could have gotten through the Math classes.) By the way, she eventually gave me homework and very helpful tools to add to my anxiety tool chest.

During therapy, we reached the point where I had to face my fear. My therapist would not be with me, I had to do this on my own. Once again, I took it to God.

I sympathized with Jacob, who wrestled to be blessed by God (Genesis 32:22-32). I wrestled to pry away the fear that kept me bound. To my surprise, something unexpected happened. The more I prayed about it the more I realized, the only person I needed with me in that battleground was my Jesus. Ding, ding, ding, the bells began to ring. The heavens had opened and angels were singing. The sun was shining and all was well in my world. All I needed was my Savior, and for the first time in my life, that was enough. Hallelujah!

Stay tuned. The story does not end here. I still had to face my fear.

My trauma was brought on by a very painful experience at a dental office when I was younger. I was given nitrous oxide, commonly known as, laughing gas. I was not administered any Novocain. To be fair, it is possible that it didn't take, and I was not sufficiently numbed. I felt every single painful sensation of them drilling and filling four teeth!

While under the influence of this gas, I lifted my hand, clenched my toes and tried to scream, but the dentist paid no mind to my discomfort. I felt extremely vulnerable under all that Novocain. I have a suspicious feeling that something inappropriate may have happened. I haven't been able to unblock a lot of the memories associated with that state of mind. Yet, the Lord has assured me that I don't need to know all the specifics of what occurred because He knew. He was there and healing would come.

God showed me that I could not live a life of true freedom without facing this giant. When you allow God into your fears, and you give Him the reigns, He will surprise your socks off! Was it easy to overcome the terror of that visit with the dentist? No. Mouth pain and the bigger fear of losing my teeth pushed me forward to make an appointment. This time I did not cancel it.

What had changed? Looking back, it was the idea that as someone younger and naive, I felt I had no say. My voice and my ability to advocate for myself were blatantly disregarded. IT WAS STOLEN FROM ME. As an adult, I have a voice. A voice to say, "Stop, it hurts," and someone would listen. Armed with this knowledge, I chose to find a dentist that would be sympathetic to my needs.

In the waiting room, I did diaphragmatic breathing exercises (You will learn those in Chapter 5). I looked at the Scriptures on my phone to calm myself. While waiting to be called, I laid out a fleece as

Gideon did. You can find the story of Gideon in Judges 6:11-40. He was a timid man. We first hear of Gideon when The Angel of the Lord finds him hiding from the Midianites in a wine press. These Midianites were ruthless. Whenever the Israelites planted their crops, they would intentionally destroy them. They would steal or kill their animals and leave them with nothing. A prophet had told the Israelites God wanted them to go to battle against these intruders.

The angel of the Lord greeted Gideon in the wine press as, "Mighty Warrior." Wow! This was an odd thing to say to a man who was shaking in his sandals. God told him He would use him to battle their enemies! How crazy is that! Gideon began making excuses that he belonged to the weakest clan and that he was the least in his family. What Gideon did not understand was that God does not see us as the scared little mice we think we are. He sees us as the valiant warriors He has called us to be. We just need to believe it and act on it.

Gideon needed confirmation that God would give him victory over his enemies. He laid out a wool fleece and asked God to allow the evening dew to be found only on the fleece, and none to be found on the ground. The man was asking for a miracle. He wanted to be sure that if he went to battle, he would win. When God answered that miracle, he asked for a second miracle. Gideon like us, wanted to have a 100 percent, iron-clad guarantee that God would have his back in the battle against the Midianites. This time the dew would be all over the ground, but the fleece would be bone dry. Guess what? God answered both times to calm his fears.

Back to my fleece… I had asked the Lord if this was the right dental place for me, there would be Christian music playing. Filling out the endless pages of paperwork, (you'd think you were going off to war or something, Geesh!) I heard ONE Christian song play. The rest of the time, the room was filled with modern, upbeat music playing. That one worship song was just the kind of confirmation my soul needed. It assured me that I would come out on the other side of that PATIENTS ONLY door, stronger. God showed me that it was the enemy who was responsible for the horror film playing in my mind. When my name was called, I wanted the earth to swallow me. I mustered up the nerve, walked to the chair my nightmares were made of and sat down. I struggled through the x-rays. Try having that apparatus in your mouth when your jaw is throbbing from TMJ pain. The hygienist examination came next. Personally, for me, this was the worst, but it was made tolerable with numbing jell. The actual dental check-up was quick, unfortunately, it revealed bad news. I had to return for two deep-scale cleanings. Yikes! None of the deep cleanings were enjoyable. I stayed focused on Jesus through the worship music resounding in my earbuds. Additionally, I used my voice as well as hand signals to communicate my needs. I had a compassionate, skilled hygienist, who was sympathetic to my phobia. This time around, it was I who made the decisions when to continue or when to take a break. It felt so freeing to be an active participant in my oral health care. Today, I am the proud owner of an electric toothbrush.

Friend, if you think you have lost your voice due to some traumatic experience, you haven't. Jesus has it. He's been holding it for you all along. He has been keeping it safe and secure for such a time as this. It is time for you to use that voice again. The voice that shouts, 'I want to get out of Fearville now!'

WORKBOOK PAGE

List three fears that you want to work on. List them in the order of importance or urgency.

Fear 1. _____

Fear 2._____

Fear 3. _____

Do you believe you have lost your voice, if so, why?

_____

_____

_____

What other lies have you been believing?

_____

_____

_____

What positive steps can you take to get your voice back?

_____

_____

_____

TRUTH FROM THE HONESTY BOX

PROCRASTINATION IS NOT YOUR FRIEND

Facing fears takes preparation. It does not happen from one day to the next. It may take therapy, as in the case of my severe dental phobia. Desire is good. I applaud your desire to want to get out of Fearville. That is a good first step. A good second step is practicing all the coping strategies outlined in this book. Now we are up to step three. You must act. Not acting on this, is equivalent to standing in front of an open door, but not walking through it.

No amount of preparation, therapy sessions, or tools, would have worked if I had made the appointment but never showed up. I had to get in my car and drive to the dental office. I had to park and walk in. Each small step I took got me closer to sitting in that chair and opening my mouth. No matter how many self-care books you read or podcasts you watch, unless you do what you are afraid to do, you will always remain frozen in your fear.

You must understand that procrastination is not your friend. When I called for my dental appointment, they had an appointment the following morning. I took a deep breath and took the appointment. Taking the quickest appointment did two things: it gave me less time to hyper-focus on my fear and didn't allow me any time to cancel without having to pay a stiff cancellation fee. The best part, I had only one sleepless night to worry about instead of weeks of torture.

WORKBOOK PAGE 1a

Sit in the Honesty Box. Below are some steps you can take when facing your fear:

Don't Procrastinate

Face your fear as soon as possible. If it is something that requires planning, set a date on your calendar. Place the calendar where you can see it every day.

I will face my fear on _____. (Date)

Taking this step will bring more anxiety. (You don't have to like it, to do it.)

Don't wait for perfect timing.

There is an old Cuban saying that I grew up hearing, *Cuando estas sentado en el caballo, no tienes otra*. When you are already sitting on a horse, you have no choice, except to ride.

Giddy up!

WORKBOOK PAGE 1b

RANTING SPACE

This will be your ranting and raving sheet. Write, draw, paint, or do a collage. It does not matter how you express how you feel about facing your fear, as long as you do. Get out of your system all those ugly feelings!

WORKBOOK PAGE 1c

If I face my fear(s)...

Circle all that applies or add your own:

I could go where I want.   I would be exercising my rights.

I could feel better about myself.   I would have freedom.

I would be less sick.   I would trust more,

I would keep healthy boundaries.   I would accomplish my dreams.

_____   _____

_____   _____

_____   _____

_____   _____

ACCOUNTABILTY PARTNER
(Optional)

Find an **Accountability Partner**. It can be a family member, a trusted friend, or a therapist.

Whoever you choose has to understand your situation fully.

Find someone who you know would want you to succeed and will be cheering you the whole way to the finish line.

This individual will become your truth teller. He or she will be honest and will tell you when you are making excuses or sitting idle in your fear and not progressing.

Don't expect them to carry you through this. That is not their job. Their job is to motivate you not coddle you.

Don't call or text them 24 hours a day. You need to do this on your own. Trust God will be by your side.

Pray.

Once you decide, make sure you share the next page with them so they too can understand the level of commitment you are requiring to overcome your fear.

ACCOUNTABLITY RULES AND CONTRACT

Name:_____   Date:_____

I will do my part by reading and doing the exercises assigned.

I will respect the advice and suggestion that come from my Accountability Partner.

I will be honest and transparent with my Accountability Partner.

I will work with my Accountability Partner to find solutions to fix or correct any problems that arise.

I will not expect perfection from my Accountability Partner. I will understand they are human and have their own struggles and life commitments. They cannot be available 24/7.

I will adhere to set times and dates that are mutually agreed upon.

Accountability Partner Name:_____

I will do my best to cheer and motivate.

I will not coddle but encourage.

I will be involved by providing a sounding board and safe place where the named person above can feel secure to share openly.

I will keep all conversations confidential.

I will abstain from judgment but show compassion.

I will adhere to set times and dates that are mutually agreed upon.

_____   _____

  Participant   Signature   Accountability Partner

HAVE I NOT COMMANDED YOU?

BE STRONG AND COURAGEOUS.

DO NOT BE AFRAID;

DO NOT BE DISCOURAGED,

FOR THE LORD YOUR GOD

WILL BE WITH

YOU

WHEREVER YOU GO.

JOSHUA 1:9

NOTES

STEP 5 USE YOUR TOOLS

TRUTH FROM THE HONESTY BOX
A PERSON WITH ANXIETY DIES
A THOUSAND DEATHS BEFORE THEY DIE

In 2020, the COVID Pandemic affected countless people. I lost my best friend, my father-in-law, and many close friends to this beast. The lockdown brought on more confusion and isolation. Everywhere you turned there was a reminder of the ugly C. Between the media, the masks, the sanitizing, and the six feet protocols, it was like living in a minefield. I was in a constant state of panic. I felt like any step in the wrong direction, could be my last. I believed it was my job to stay one step ahead of the chaos. But was it really my job? What about God?

While the COVID death toll numbers went down, my anxiety continued to skyrocket. I started scrutinizing my every ache, breath, and strange bodily sensation for signs of an impending untimely death. Reaching for the pulse oximeter became an everyday event. It did not matter that my immune system had handled COVID well, or that my labs were exemplary. Fear kidnaps our logic and hurls it back into the darkness of Fearville. There we can die a thousand deaths in the theater of our adrenaline-soaked imagination!

When anxiety strikes, it creates a barrier separating us from the present. My fear of COVID had separated me from life. It kept me from being present and engaged. Our time on this earth is limited. I was wasting opportunities to make lasting memories with my family and friends. I became a doormat, allowing fear of COVID to trample me, but I had had enough!

The beauty of it all was that even through the panic, God was working. He was using my mustard seed-sized faith to remind me that my victim mentality was not going to work. My family needed me and I could not stay in bed in a fetal position waiting for COVID to disappear.

I had to push myself to see fear for the schoolyard bully it was. When I did, I became angry. My wishy-washy, whiny, tear-soaked prayers, changed. They became bold, authoritative prayers. I became proactive. I relied on a kick-butt friend who didn't let me give up. I found out that to stay mentally balanced I had to stay hungry and angry. Hungry for more of God's Word. Hungry for more faith, and angry enough to reclaim what the enemy had stolen from me, my peace.

Are you sick and tired of your annoying fears getting in the way of your life? Then drop the defeated attitude and see yourself as an angry, hungry, warrior. Get ready to fight!

"The Spirit you received does not make you slaves, so that you live in fear again; rather, the Spirit you received brought about your adoption to sonship. And by him we cry," Abba Father" (Romans 8:15).

WORKBOOK PAGE

Find 3 Scriptures that can help you feel protected. God's promises can calm your anxiety.

Write them below:

Scripture

1_____

_____

_____

Scripture

2_____

_____

_____

Scripture

3_____

_____

_____

Pick one to memorize.

TRUTH FROM THE HONESTY BOX
PRAYER IS THE MOST IMPORTANT TOOL

We are in warfare! That's right I said warfare. The enemy is anything but meek or timid. "Your enemy the devil prowls around like a roaring lion looking for someone to devour" (1 Peter 5:8). When you call on Jesus, those demons cannot touch you. To rebuke the enemy, we don't need long dissertations full of hot air. Remember the imaginary balloon? What we need is strong words that are based on the authority given to us by God's Word. Did you get that Warrior?

One night when my three-year-old was sick, I was awakened by the most horrendous, satanic dream. My daughter was thrashing in her bed, unable to attain calm sleep. I was petrified. I could not move. A dark presence was all around us. Fear was engulfing me. For the sake of my daughter, I had to confront this sinister force.

Between 3:00 and 6:00 AM, I was thrust into intense Spiritual Warfare. As I covered us in prayer, I felt myself getting stronger and more determined to keep on fighting. I did not stop praying until God gave me the sign that it was over. Once that happened, my baby girl settled down and slept without a sound. We were both able to rest in our Heavenly Father's peace.

During the difficult weeks of medical testing that followed, my child was hedged in prayer. Prayers were answered when the diagnosis came back as something minor that would not alter her quality of life.

Prayer is the most versatile weapon we have. It can be used at any time, any place, and for as long as it takes. I never thought I could pray without ceasing for hours. I was not a veteran prayer warrior and this encounter was not up my alley. It was a skirmish meant for the pros, but when faced with this kind of fear, we have Jesus to back us up.

No, in all these things we are more than conquerors through him who loves us. For I am convinced that neither death, nor life, neither angels nor demons, neither present or future, nor any powers, neither height nor depth, nor anything else in all creation, will be able to separate us from the love of God that is in Christ Jesus our Lord" (Romans 8:37-39).

Fear sometimes disguises itself under the cover of logic. "If it quacks like a duck, and walks like a duck, then it must be a duck." But this does not always prove true, especially in dealing with the physical sensations you will experience when you are in the clutches of a panic or anxiety attack.

In 2018, it was estimated that 80 percent of persons who ended up in the Emergency Room with chest pain thinking they are having a true cardiopulmonary emergency are not. They believe they are having a heart attack or they have some other incurable disease. When the doctor administers tests, including imaging, and other diagnostic tools, the result seldom shows a heart problem. 8

Unless you are a medical professional, DO NOT GOOGLE YOUR SYMPTOMS. As an untrained person, you will not be able to distinguish between benign anxiety symptoms and something else. Most sites have a habit of catastrophizing. Before you know it, you will have sentenced yourself to an early grave.

"Fear begins as an impulse in our brain that excites the sympathetic nerves to stimulate various regions (skin) and organs..." Dr. Claire Weekes. 9

Googling symptoms makes it easy for the enemy to mess with your mind. Our Creator gave us very complex bodies. Fear can work for our benefit when we are faced with real danger. The rush of adrenaline helps us to move faster. In the flight or fight stage our bodies become prepared to either fight against the danger or run away from the danger. When we feel relaxed, we stroll around, unaware of our body's mechanisms. *Normally we do not feel our body functioning, because the parasympathetic nerves hold the sympathetic nerves in check. (Weekes)*

I am not stating that you should ignore red flags. Go ahead and knock on all the medical doors until someone gives you a proper diagnosis. I did much knocking before someone diagnosed me. Keep in mind that panic attacks can mimic anything from a head cold to a heart attack. I am not going to go into the science behind it, but I do encourage you to learn all you can about the cause, aggravating factors, and possible treatments available. You have permission to google that information. Knowing the truth will set you free to deal with the facts.

No longer will the Fearville monsters intimidate you. You will feel more confident, therefore you will be able to discuss options with your medical professionals more openly. By acquiring more knowledge, you can help others that may be suffering too.

TRUTH FROM THE HONESTY BOX

IT ALL BEGINS WITH A THOUGHT

"Finally, brothers whatever is true, whatever is right, whatever is noble, whatever is lovely, whatever is admirable--if anything is excellent or praiseworthy--think about such things"
(Philippians 4:8).

Thoughts can be our friends or our enemies. Positive thoughts help us to see the world in a good light. Negative thoughts produce negative feelings that create anxiety.

Sometimes fear comes out of the blue. Or so we think. It could be that you are sitting there relaxing when your heart begins to beat fast for no apparent reason. What could be causing it? If you are prone to anxiety like me, this can start a chain of irrational thoughts. Those heart palpitations will cause the logical part of your brain to take a detour down an unsettling path. This can happen with any anxiety symptom, but for clarity, we will use heart palpitations as an example.

Ex: Ba bump, ba bump, ba bump! That's the sound of my heart racing.

My thoughts:

"Something is wrong with me!"
"I am sick!"
"I have a heart problem!"

Maybe your mind is not as dramatic as mine, but you get the picture. If we backtrack, we can find that even though there was nothing presently endangering me, it was one thought that started this whole mess. Here is where we need to apply Truth. In 2 Corinthians 10:5, we are told to take every thought captive.

But why? Because God knows that if we let our stressed-out minds wander, it always leads us to destruction and separation from Him. Another thing these thoughts do, they dull our ability to see God's goodness in our lives.

Mental health therapists tell us that we can control our thoughts by *redirecting, dismissing, or changing* them. They are not wrong in this. In Romans 12:2, God's Word tells us we must renew our minds. Still, I have never seen a Taking Thoughts Captive 101 class in college. It's not something taught in the formative years or even modeled by most parents. Thinking is accepted as something we just do, like breathing.

What you have learned so far:

- God is not the author of fear.

- It comes from the enemy, Satan.

- There are negative emotions such as shame, guilt, depression, unforgiveness, and worthlessness that hold you hostage in Fearville and feed your fears.

To understand how our brains affects our fears, let us return to the example of heart palpitations. From the moment my heart started to pound, what was the first thought that went through my mind?

- *Something is wrong with me!*

The alarm goes off: Houston, we have a problem!

- *I am sick!*

I have decided that this rapid heartbeat could only mean that I am no longer a healthy individual.

- *I am having a heart problem!*

Here I am self-diagnosing. A big no-no. I have Health Anxiety so anything health related can send me into a frenzy.

- *I am going to die!*

Now I am playing God and foretelling the future. A very grim future of my own making.

You can see this whole thought process is like a snowball rolling down a hill. Each thought made the anxiety grow bigger and bigger until it could not be controlled any longer. Simultaneously, my body was reacting to all the stress producing more thoughts and adding a host of new symptoms including sweats, chills, vision disturbances, throat tightness, breathing difficulties, etc. Can you see how quickly my mind took me from heart palpitations to my funeral?

If it is proven by science and most importantly by God that we can stop those thoughts. How do we do it?

POSITIVE THOUGHTS THAT HAVE WORKED FOR ME:

- *Ba bump, Ba bump…My heart is racing*

Ignore it - Concentrate on something physical that will keep your mind off it. Example: Pay bills, cook, take a soothing bath, or a warm shower, take a walk.

Validate it -"Yes, my heart is beating a little fast." I am stating the obvious, but not adding anything else to it.

- *Something is wrong with me!*

Validation and Action - "My heart is beating a little fast. A fast-paced heart means I am anxious. I can do some breathing exercises to calm down."

- *I have a heart problem!*

Reality Check - "I do not have a medical degree. What I have is anxiety that I can reduce by using my self-care tools." (I have added tools for you to use on page 91.)

- *I am going to die!*

Truth: Now I am playing God.

"This is a distorted thought. It is a bald-faced lie from the enemy. Only God knows when I am going to die."

If you get to this point, it is an indication that your anxiety is not letting up. It is time not only to continue to use your tools but to reframe your thoughts with a more aggressive positive thinking response. This will take more deliberate work on your part.

Remind yourself of the truth. God is with me even at this moment. What I am feeling is anxiety. It is caused by the chemicals running throughout my body and the lies the enemy wants me to believe.

Stay in the present. Don't allow your mind to go to a regretful past, or a defeating, self-created future.

Remind yourself of positive outcomes. Last time you didn't die. You are a survivor because you have survived this before.

When anxiety won't release you:

Ride the wave. Feel the symptoms but don't shrink back from them or try to stop them.

Be gentle with yourself. Even after it is over, it is not the time to lecture yourself.

Congratulate yourself. Treat yourself to a nap, a treat, or something relaxing.

Review the event. Later on in the day, or the next day, take inventory. What symptoms did you have? What made them worse?

WORKBOOK PAGE 1a

ANXIETY BUSTER PRACTICE

Pick a symptom that bothers you when you are anxious.

Pick a number from a scale of 1 through 10 (1 being tolerable and 10 being the worst you have ever experienced.)

Write the corresponding information in the blanks below.

Symptom

_____

Scale #_____

Write down the **FIRST** negative thought that goes through your head. Then write a positive thought you can use to lessen the anxiety.

Negative Thought

_____

Positive Thought

_____

Scale #_____

WORKBOOK PAGE 1b

Did the competing positive thought bring down your anxiety?

Yes or No

If your answer is No, you can choose another Positive thought.

Continue adding positive thoughts until the anxiety scale number goes down.

Positive Thought
_____

Scale#_____

Positive Thought_____

Scale#_____

Positive Thought_____

Scale#_____

Positive Thought _____

Scale#_____

Positive Thought_____

Scale#_____

"Do not be conformed to this world, but be transformed by the renewal of your mind, that by testing you may discern what is the will of God, what is good and acceptable and perfect" (Romans 12:2.)

On the following page you will get a sampling of practical tools that have worked for me. Tools are like shoes, not all size fits all. So try them out and see which ones work best for you.

TOOL BOX

Disclaimer: I am not a licensed doctor or therapist. Please always consult with your physician to determine if any of the exercises or suggestions outlined in this book are suitable for your specific condition.

DIAPHRAGMATIC BREATHING: We don't breathe correctly when we are anxious. This can make us take shallow breaths and even hyperventilate.

Take a deep breath through your nose: Place your hand on your belly. You should feel your belly pushing outward.

Hold your breath: For this exercise you will hold your breath for a count of two. As you get better at this, you can increase the time depending on your need or mood.

Exhale: Place your hand on your belly. This time you should feel your stomach retracts. Purse your lips and let the air come out of your mouth slowly. Don't stop until all the air you breathed in comes out. (You should feel your shoulders relax.)

(There are many different breathing techniques available you can try. Google: Breathing Techniques for Anxiety)

Mental Health professionals use grounding techniques as mental distractions to help redirect your thoughts away from distressing feelings and back to the present. (University Hospital) 10

STAYING IN THE PRESENT: Knowing God is with you, use your five senses to remain present and not let your mind wander. Pay close attention to your surroundings and environment. There will always be something to focus on, an aroma or smell, noise even in the quiet, and tangible objects to touch.

- What do you see?

- What do you hear?

- What do you smell?

- What do you feel?

WORKBOOK PAGE

What do you see? Look at your surroundings. Describe them.

_____

_____

What do you hear? Unless you are in a soundproof room, there will be sound.

_____

_____

What do you smell? There is always an odor to pick up.

_____

_____

What do you feel? Touch something and describe how it feels. Is it soft, leathery, or silky...

_____

_____

SHOCKING YOUR SYSTEM:

Drink cold water or warm soothing tea.

Submerge hands, face, or body in icy water. The colder the better. Even an ice pack on your wrists or neck will work.

Taste something sour or spicy.

Smell Essential oils. They can be put in diffusers. Drops can be placed in your cupped hands and smelled or applied directly to the skin. Always check the directions before using them.

DISTRACTIONS AND MEDITATION:

Worship music: Even reading the lyrics will help because they are typically based on Scripture.

Sing: Sometimes in the middle of an episode I can't even remember my favorite songs, but I can recall childhood songs.

Example: Jesus Loves Me. This Little Light of Mine. Row Row Row your Boat, Old Mc. Donald

Recite by Rote Memory: Scriptures, ABCs, 1,2,3's

*It could be something simple or as complex as medical terminology or solving Algebraic equations. The idea is to keep your brain engaged in something else. Preferably something of great importance like God's Word.

Therefore, I tell you, do not worry about your life, what you will eat or drink; or about your body, what you will wear. Is not life more than food, and the body more than clothes? Look at the birds of the air; they do not sow or reap or store away in barns, and yet your heavenly Father feeds them. Are you not much more valuable than they? Can any one of you by worrying add a single hour to your life? (Matthew 6:25-27).

THANKFULNESS:

Thankfulness as a tool? Are you kidding? No, I am not. Being thankful should not be a one-time event, like Thanksgiving. For the Christian, the word *"Christian"* should be synonymous with the word, *"Thankful."* We are to be the most thankful people on the planet. Sadly, what usually comes out of our mouths are groans and grumbles, especially if we are having an anxiety filled day.

 In our anxiety and worry, we don't take into consideration that we owe a mountain of gratitude to God. The creator of everything, did not have to create us or this beautiful planet. He owes us nothing. Nevertheless, He took the time to fashion us humans in His image. To put the icing on the cake, He sent His son to save us from ourselves and has promised eternal life to those who love Him. There is no way we could ever repay God for His abundant grace and mercy!

Science has proven that being thankful can have favorable results in people with anxiety and depression. The daily practice of gratitude releases feel good hormones like dopamine and serotonin. These are considered to be neurotransmitters that are responsible for our positive emotions. If you continue practicing thankfulness, it is said that it can help reduce negative emotions and strengthen your neural pathways. As well, it is proven that anxiety and gratitude cannot coexist in the brain at the same time. (You can find more detailed information on the internet about this subject.)

For those of you who are trapped in Fearville, life is covered by an opaque veil of unsettledness and negativity that hides all the good life has to offer. Therefore, it will take a deliberate search on your part to find it. You might argue that it is impossible to find anything to be thankful for. Everything that could go wrong, goes wrong for you. Yes, we all have had those days where the dog poops on the carpet you just cleaned, the sole of your shoe comes off on the way to work, and your car breaks down in the middle of rush hour traffic.

Days like that seem endless. In those days when I just cannot get out of my own head, this is the slogan that brings me back.

FACT: *There is always something to be **THANKFUL** for **BECAUSE** it can always be worse.*

I know you won't take that statement at face value, because trust is not your default mechanism yet. That is why we are going to peel back the layers of this statement and see if it can be trusted.

As you hold this book, you are using your hands. You are using your eyes to see the letters. Likewise, you are using your brain to decode the information you are reading. You have something many don't have. Someone who is blind cannot see this book. A person who has no arms or hands cannot hold this book. Brain injured or intellectually delayed individuals cannot process this much information. You are blessed with sight, physical ability, and an intelligent brain. Don't you think that is something to be thankful for?

You may despise your anxiety, and have thoughts like, "My anxiety is the worst!" Really? Hm...I think its time to put that statement to a test.

Do you prefer having an inoperable tumor or anxiety? No contest, right? In the light of an inoperable tumor, anxiety would not seem as detrimental. If you live in a tiny apartment, you may complain, while someone who is homeless would give anything to have a safe place to live away from the harsh elements in the streets. It all boils down to *perspective*. Or as they say, "Is your glass half full or half empty?"

There are so many things in life to be thankful for, It would take multiple life times to count them all. We probably run out of numbers if that was possible!

Here is a list to help you get to a place of thankfulness. This will make you accustomed to seeing things from a more beneficial perspective.

Being thankful for what our five senses can pick up. Anything you can experience with your five senses that brings you joy is something to be thankful for. Without our five senses we would live very limited lives.

Being thankful for our bodies and the jobs they do. Our bodies have multiple organs and systems that work to bring us quality of life. Without the proper work of these organs and systems our lives could be compromised.

Being thankful for those who love us or meaningful relationships. Whether it's friends. family, co-workers, or love interests, etc., people in our lives can be a gift that bring us comfort and joy. Even a server with a pleasant smile and good work ethic can be a gift compared to someone who is grouchy and lazy.

Being thankful for nature and the world around us. The beautiful sunsets painted with golds and pinks, or the breathtaking views of the Grand Canyon, to name a few. In the USA we complain about politics and how the country is not run the way we think it should be run. However, even when things aren't perfect, we have so much to be thankful for. We have brave soldiers to defend our country. We have people in government still willing to fight for what is right.

Being thankful for having our physical needs met. We have clean drinking water to quench our thirst. We have food in the grocery stores and our refrigerators to fill our bellies. We have electricity that provides heat and air condition, and so much more.

If you get stuck in your quest to find something to be thankful for, close your eyes. Imagine you live in an impoverished third world country, and have many illnesses. Plus, there has been a war, and nobody even knows you are alive.

Now weigh your present life against that one. We can get so tied up in our own dark, stinky, mindset that we forget how blessed we are.

Let them give thanks to the Lord for his unfailing love and his wonderful deeds for mankind, for he satisfies the thirsty and fills the hungry with good things (Psalm 107:8-9).

Fire fighters don't just get up one day and start running into burning buildings. They spend many hours preparing and practicing. They first practice in a non-threatening environment, where the risk is calculated and easily controlled. They repeat dressing in their firefighter uniforms, carrying the heavy hoses, and running in and out of the fire. Timing is paramount for firefighters. Every minute counts. That is why they will practice until they are able to respond quicker before they have to put out an uncontrolled fire or save someone's life.

It's the same with using your tools. You are to practice using them when you are calm, cool and collected. Thus, you will be practicing in a controlled, calculated, risk-free environment. You will continue practicing until it gets easy. Then when anxiety strikes, putting the tools to work will be familiar to you. With daily practice, it will become an automatic response when you experience anxiety.

WORKBOOK PAGE 1a

Write down what you are thankful for in each category:

My five senses.

I am thankful that I can see _____

I am thankful that I can hear _____

I am thankful that I can taste _____

I am thankful that I can smell _____

I am thankful that I can touch _____

I am thankful for my body that can _____

_____

I am thankful for _____ who helps me with

_____

I am thankful for God's creation, specially thankful for:

_____

_____

_____

WORKBOOK PAGE 1b

I am thankful for having this physical need met: Ex. I am thankful that I can eat my favorite dessert.

_____

_____

_____

The next lines are for you to put down what you are thankful for right now at this moment.

_____

_____

_____

From the moment you wake up to the moment you go to bed, make a list daily of what you are thankful for. Blessings are all around us. It is up to us to recognize them.

WORKBOOK PAGE 1c

In the Anxiety Busting Practice page, you practiced reducing the scale number by replacing a negative thought with a competing positive thought. Now you are going to fight your anxiety and fear with both barrels loaded. To your competing thought you will be adding a tool from the Tool Box page.

Practice Using Multiple Tools To Reduce Anxiety

Anxiety Scale (1 through 10, 1 being light anxiety and 10 total panic)

*Negative thought:

_____

Scale # _____

Competing Positive Thought:

_____

Tool used:

_____

Scale #_____

*Negative thought:

_____

Scale #_____

Competing Positive thought:

_____

Tool used:

_____

Scale #_____

*Negative thought:

_____

Scale #_____

Competing Positive thought:

_____

Tool used:

_____

Scale #_____

*Negative thought:

_____

Scale #_____

Competing Positive thought:

_____

Tool used:

_____

Scale #_____

Practice this until it becomes second nature.

TRUTH FROM THE HONESTY BOX
ANXIETY TOOLS ARE USELESS IF YOU
CAN'T GET TO THEM FAST

You have learned a lot of different strategies and tools to use in this book. But an anxious mind is notorious for forgetting everything that has been read. During a panic or anxiety attack, the brain gets easily muddled and you are blessed if you can remember your name let alone instructions. Having your tools where you can reach them quickly, is the antidote to slow down or even stop an attack before it begins.

In this technologically advanced world, we never have to be without our tools. You will be using your beloved smartphone. Inside these mechanical boxes, you will find some kind of a note-taking app. If you don't have one built into your phone, you can download it from your app store.

This is the key to the treasure box. Here you can store all your tools and when an anxiety or panic emergency arises, you will have all you need right in the palm of your hand. You can add, edit, and delete tools as needed. You can add helpful links, write encouraging reminders to yourself, and download worship music, or scripture references. You can even journal about how your day is going. If you don't understand technology, you can still use a regular notebook, but make it small enough to carry in your pocket or purse.

I SOUGHT THE LORD,

AND HE ANSWERED ME AND DELIVERED ME
FROM ALL MY FEARS.

THOSE WHO LOOK TO HIM ARE RADIANT;

THEIR FACES ARE NEVER COVERED WITH
SHAME.

PSALM 34:4-5

NOTES

STEP 6 FOCUS ON FREEDOM

TRUTH FROM THE HONESTY BOX

THE *WHAT IFS'* WILL KILL YOUR PROGRESS

By now I hope you understand that you cannot predict the future. The future is and always will be in God's hands. I know you are eager to leave Fearville. You have done a lot of hard work and congratulations are in order. But before we throw the confetti, you must check your upstairs thought factory. Did you know that all along there has been a tiny, nasty, slimy, bug-eyed *WHAT IFS'* monster hiding in your brain? We can't let you leave Fearville with that pest running around in there. We are going to exterminate it!

In Matthew 6:25-34, Jesus tells us not to worry about anything. He adds that worrying cannot add a single hour to our life. Inside these verses there is also a reminder that each day comes with worries of its own, It is wise not to borrow worries ahead of time.

Anticipation of a panic attack is worse than the actual attack. With the *WHAT IFS'* in place, our imagination can take wind and cause us to visualize the worse possible scenario. That little monster that usually nips at our feet can become as large as Godzilla!

Dwelling on *"What if it happens again?"* is exactly how you can bring on the increasing severity and frequency of the attacks. God does not want the *WHAT IFS'* monster to boss you around. He does not want constant dread plaguing your every thought. His plans for you are not for you to keep hiding under the covers for days. You can exterminate this monster by clinging to God's promises.

The mind governed by the flesh is death, but the mind governed by the Spirit is life and peace" (Romans 8:6).

It is a waste of time to worry about the WHAT IFS'. The *WHAT IFS'* rarely happen and if they do, we usually learn something from them.

My life has been full of terrible misfortunes most of which never happened. Michel de Montaigne 10

When we worry, we are not living. We are at a standstill, waiting for the carousel of life to stop so we can get on. As you know, this carousel will not even slow down. Therefore, we sit in Fearville like spectators on the sidelines watching our lives pass us by. We forgo all our dreams because of fear and live less productive and satisfying lives. Oh, and the *WHAT IFS'* monster, it will keep growing and growing!

WORKBOOK PAGE

Look at this list. Which *WHAT IFS' Monsters* are hiding in your mind?

If it happens again ___

If I fail __

If it hurts ___

If they don't like me ___

If I hurt someone ___

If I look, sound, or act foolish ___

If I freak out ___

If they don't believe me ___

If I panic again ___

If I make a scene ___

If they don't understand ___

Feel free to add any *WHAT IFS'* Monsters that I missed.

_____

_____

What have you learned from fighting the *WHAT IFS'* Monsters?

_____

_____

_____

TRUTH FROM THE HONESTY BOX

YOU CAN'T LEAVE FEARVILLE WITH UNFORGIVENESS IN YOUR HEART

If you think you can leave Fearville while carrying unforgiveness in your heart, think again. To leave, you must travel light. Leave behind anything that stunts your emotional growth and lowers your self-esteem. If you don't, the memories will become chains. They will bind you and return you to the fear and insecurity that put you in Fearville in the first place.

All the hurts that are lingering in the past affects our present more than we know. The past can shape us. Words and actions from unpleasant memories can hinder us and cause us to develop defective coping mechanisms that are detrimental to our wholeness.

Forgiveness and restoration go hand and hand. You can't work on establishing who God says you are, if you are still resentful for what was done or said to you in the past. In Jesus, we can find rest from all troublesome memories and repressed emotions.

Sometimes it is necessary to make actual contact with whoever hurt you. If the person is still around, you can set up a time to meet or speak on the phone. Let them know they hurt you, but that you are willing to forgive them. Depending on the situation, this brave act on your part, could become the beginning of a reconciliation.

There are other situations that would make it impossible or dangerous to make contact. Sometimes the person is deceased or they are too toxic to be around. Protecting your mental and physical health must come first. God wants you to be safe.

The decision how you go about this is up to you. I suggest you turn to the Holy Spirit for guidance. To get out of Fearville, you will need to forgive regardless if you do it in private or in person.

In some instances, due to trauma, PTSD, or other mental blockages, you might not remember much of the event, yet you know there was someone who hurt you. There are therapists who specialize in helping you access those repressed memories if you feel it will help you heal.

I must confess it bothered me a lot that I could not see in my mind's eye all the details or even the face of the person who was responsible for my dental phobia. As much as I tried to remember there was a fog that surrounded that event, but I did not seek targeted therapy to unlock the memories.

In prayer, during a self-care study group, God showed me a two-story building. Jesus was holding my hand and pointing to it. I had been praying for the courage to face my past, so I could face a similar situation in the present. In the vision, I thought Jesus wanted me to go into the building. But just as I was getting ready to go in, He stopped me. Jesus told me that because He was there when it happened, I did not need to face it again. He told me to trust Him to hold that ugly memory for me. Even though I could not see the person clearly, I still needed to forgive them. In my case, the healing happened not by reliving the painful memory but by forgiving the one who caused it.

If you feel God is calling you to go this route, here is a prayer you can pray:

Jesus, I hand over my need to relive the past. I know you have seen the wounds that have been made by careless words and actions from those I trusted. Those words and actions used against me have no authority over me any longer. I place them at the foot of the cross. I choose to forgive all wrongdoing that was done to me, and move toward a healthier me. The me you created before this event ever took place. I am set free from the bondage of resentment and hatred and any spiritual ties that create fear and oppression. I let go of the bitterness and pain and allow your Holy Spirit to wash me clean. I am worthy of being treated with respect and love and I will walk in that knowledge and authority from this point forward. In Jesus' name, Amen.

The Israelites spend 40 years wandering in the desert. This was due to the fear of being without food or water. This fear kept them from believing the miracles they had witnessed with their own eyes. God time and time again had provided for all their needs. Fear ushered in unbelief where doubting became a way of life. This doubting caused Korah, and his buddies their lives. He doubted Moses was the chosen one of God. He created rebellion in the camp and as a result, God had the earth swallow him up. (Paraphrased from Numbers Chapter 16).

God does not punish us because we are fearful. He does not have to. We do it to ourselves. We punish ourselves by living smaller and not living life to the fullest. You can't tell me that living in fear benefits you in any way. Fear takes away from your joy and peace. It can create rifts in relationships, cause loss of employment, and decreases productivity. Fear engages you in a perpetual game of cat-and-mouse. Always running, hiding, and never chasing. We stop chasing dreams, we stop chasing success, and we become accustomed to being slaves.

Being slaves to fear, that was the downfall of the Israelites. They were conditioned back in Egypt to live in fear. Fear of being beaten, fear of being imprisoned or killed. Even when God set them free from Egypt, they still had the mindset of slaves. Fear clung to them like the fetters they had worn.

Perhaps escaping Fearville may seem as risky and daunting as escaping Egypt to you. Don't let it stop you from reaching your promised land. Just like God was with the Israelites in the desert (the unknown), God will be with you as you step out in faith. He will show you miracles and open seas where you can walk unafraid right through them. (Read Exodus.)

WORKBOOK PAGE

What punishment are you experiencing due to living in fear?

_____

_____

_____

How is this punishment affecting the quality of your life?

_____

_____

_____

What steps can you take to stop this?

_____

_____

_____

TRUTH FROM THE HONESTY BOX

FEAR CAN HAPPEN OUTSIDE OF FEARVILLE

What if I get scared or anxious again? It's not a matter of *if*, it's a matter of *when*. In this life, even if you exterminated the WHAT IFS monster, there will be times that no matter how prepared or prayed up you are, it will still bring some level of anxiety or fear.

Being out of Fearville does not guarantee that you will never feel fear again. Until we get to heaven, human beings will still be vulnerable to Earth's environment. A healthy logical fear can save your life and keep you from dangerous things. The natural alarm system built in you by your creator is a gift! The good news is now you have the tools to discern between real fear and imagined threats that want to control you.

Friend, we are getting to the end of this book. That does not mean that you are done. This is your new beginning! A chance to start Fear Less Living. You are never alone in this journey. You have God with you. He is available 24 hours a day, 7 days a week. You have this book that you can refer to. It is okay to be a little nervous. What is it like outside of Fearville you wonder? Step outside and see for yourself.

Can you see the sunlight illuminating the clear blue sky? The air is soft and caressing. The smells are inviting and pleasant. Can you feel the joy and peace deep within your soul?

I see you. You are standing there waiting. Then Jesus comes and takes your hand. He says, "My child it is time to start living the life I have prepared for you. Go. Live out your life in Fearless faith!"

TRUST IN THE LORD WITH ALL YOUR HEART,
AND
DO NOT LEAN ON YOUR OWN UNDERTANDING.
IN ALL YOUR WAYS SUBMIT TO HIM,
AND
HE WILL MAKE YOUR PATHS
STRAIGHT.

PROVERBS 3:5-6

NOTES

SCRIPTURE READING AGAINST ANXIETY

Psalm 121 Reminds you that God is in control of everything and He is your protector.

Isaiah 35:4 God will save you.

Isaiah 40:31 If you are tired and worn out this is the verse to meditate on. A promise that those who hope in the Lord will be renewed.

Zephaniah 3:17 This is a good reminder of how much you are loved. Did you know God sings because he is delighted with you?

Psalm 94:19 The antidote to Anxiety.

RESOURCES

https://www.psychologytoday.com/us/therapists

https://www.focusonthefamily.com/get-help/counseling-services-and-referrals/

National Domestic Violence Hotline 1-800-799-7233

https://www.myflfamilies.com/services/abuse/domestic-violence
(Florida)

Florida Domestic Violence Hotline 1-800-500-1119

NOTES

AN INVITATION

Do you recall a point in your life when you accepted Jesus Christ as your Lord and Savior? You may have grown up in a Christian household, know Bible verses like you know your ABCs, or hold a position in a church. Do you know you can still be lost?

My husband grew up in a Christian home and was in church every Wednesday and Sunday. Yet, after being involved in multiple ministries, he still was not saved! Say What?!?

It took the Holy Spirit filled words of a traveling worship pastor, for my husband to realize that he had dotted all the I's, and crossed all the T's but deep inside he had not made Jesus his number 1. Once the words in that concert clicked, there was no stopping him from making a public declaration of faith. He was no longer the one running his life, and it showed.

Maybe you know about Jesus and you even have a healthy fear of God. But is Jesus your number 1?

You may think, *I am not a religious person, but I am a good person. I give to charity. I help my fellow man, and do x y z... Surely God would let me into heaven, right?*

"All of us have become like one who is unclean, and all our righteous acts are like filthy rags; we all shrivel up like a leaf, and like the wind our sins sweep us away." Isaiah 64:6

I go to confession, I give to the church, I pray, I take communion. There is no Jesus and _____. God does not need a middleman. No pastor, preacher, priest, rabbi, friend, family, or love interest can save your soul. When you choose religion or any belief in place of a relationship with Jesus, you are saying His sacrifice was not enough to save you.

Jesus answered, "I am the way, the truth, and the life. No one comes to the Father except through me." John 14:6

So then am I doomed? Not unless you choose to be.

"God so loved the world, that He gave His one and only son, that whoever believes in Him should not perish but have everlasting life." John 3:16

This is the crux of Christianity. Your eternal future hangs on this verse. This is the hero coming with the cavalry to save your soul from eternal damnation. When God in the flesh, died on a cross He was not just an ordinary martyr. His death was not an injustice over which God had no control over. This was part of God's plan to ransom us from the clutches of sin.

Salvation is a free gift you can have right now.

Requirement: Childlike faith.

If you declare with your mouth, "Jesus is Lord," and believe in your heart that God raised him from the dead, you will be saved. Romans 10:9

Do you want this gift? Do you want Jesus to take full control of your life?

Yes? Then pray something like this:

Lord Jesus,
I know I am a sinner.
Please forgive me for my rebellion against you.
I want to surrender my will, my mind, and my spirit to you.
Please wash me clean of my sins and give me a fresh start.
Thank you for the gift of eternal life.
I accept it and will strive to live my life according to your Word.
In Jesus' name.
Amen.

Welcome to the family!

You can learn more about this free gift you have been given by reading the 4 Gospels, Matthew, Mark, Luke, and John. Find a church that teaches the Bible and will commit to helping you grow in your faith.

New Birth Certificate

Name_____Date: _____

END NOTES

✷ **All scripture reference is taken from the Holy Bible, New International Version, New King James, unless otherwise noted.**

1. Mayo Clinic Staff. "Positive Thinking: Stop Negative Self-Talk to Reduce Stress." *Mayo Clinic*, 3 Feb. 2022, www.mayoclinic.org/healthy-lifestyle/stress-management/in-depth/positive-thinking/art-20043950.

2. Wikipedia Contributors. "Trauma Trigger." *Wikipedia*, Wikimedia Foundation, 4 Sept. 2019, en.wikipedia.org/wiki/Trauma trigger.

3. Sharma, Ayisha, and Poonam Sachdev. "What Is a Type A Personality?" *WebMD*, 2020, www.webmd.com/balance/what-is-a-type-a-personality#091e9c5e822dcc0a-1-2. Accessed 16 Mar. 2023.

4. "Hobbit." *Wikipedia*, 15 Mar. 2023, en.wikipedia.org/wiki/Hobbit#:~:text=10.3%20Sources-. Accessed 16 Mar. 2023.

5. DiGiulio, Sarah. "What Is Gaslighting?" *NBC News*, 13 July 2018, www.nbcnews.com/better/health/what-gaslighting-how-do-you-know-if-it-s-happening- ncna890866.

6. Psychology Today. "Codependency | Psychology Today." *Www.psychologytoday.com*, 2023,

7. *Field of Dreams*. Directed by Phil Robinson Alden, Universal Pictures, 1989.

8. Musey, Paul I., et al. "Anxiety about Anxiety: A Survey of Emergency Department Provider Beliefs and Practices Regarding Anxiety-Associated Low Risk Chest Pain." *BMC Emergency Medicine*, vol. 18, no. 1, Mar. 2018, https://doi.org/10.1186/s12873-018-0161-x.

9. Weekes, Claire. *Hope and Help for Your Nerves*. Penguin, 1990.

10. Sharpe, Matthew. "Guide to the Classics: Michel de Montaigne's Essays." *The Conversation*, 2016, theconversation.com/guide-to-the-classics-michel-de-montaignes-essays-63508.

AUTHOR BIO

Christian Author, **Ileana M. Leon**, was diagnosed with panic disorder as a teenager. The focus of her writing is to bring awareness to mental health issues. She is motivated by both her personal and professional careers. As a former Paralegal and Administrative Assistant for Children and Family Services, Ileana understands the negative effects of mental health struggles.

Throughout her life, Ileana, has been the voice of countless special needs families. She has provided advocacy, education, and resource support. Her first novel, On the Edge of Truth, brought light to the impact of trauma caused by tragedy. She desires to see people who suffer from anxiety and fear be set free and live more fulfilling lives. In Fear Less Living, she shares her personal experience, as well as provides practical and faith-based approaches for the reader to find inner healing.

Ileana has contributed writings in Walking on Water, A Collection of Christian Stories and Poems, published by Westbow Press. Her novel, On the Edge of Truth, can be found on Amazon. Available both in paperback and Kindle versions.

When she is not writing or doing ministry, you can find her enjoying time with her family in sunny Florida. You can contact her at <u>Leonwrites4truth@gmail.com</u>

Made in United States
Orlando, FL
12 April 2024

45701011R00081